Series/Number 04-016

Changing Patterns of Political Beliefs: The Foreign Policy Operational Codes of J. William Fulbright, 1943-1967

KURT K. TWERASER
University of Arkansas

E.T.S.U. AT TEXARKANA LIBRARY

 SAGE PUBLICATIONS / Beverly Hills / London

Copyright © 1974 by Sage Publications, Inc.

Printed in the United States of America

All rights reserved. No part of this book may be reproduced or utilized in any form or by any means, electronic or mechanical, including photocopying, recording, or by any information storage and retrieval system, without permission in writing from the publisher.

For information address:

SAGE PUBLICATIONS, INC.
275 South Beverly Drive
Beverly Hills, California 90212

SAGE PUBLICATIONS LTD
St George's House / 44 Hatton Garden
London EC1N 8ER

International Standard Book Number 0-8039-0401-0

Library of Congress Catalog Card No. 74-80911

FIRST PRINTING

When citing a professional paper, please use the proper form. Remember to cite the correct Sage Professional Paper series title and include the paper number. One of the two following formats can be adapted (depending on the style manual used):

(1) NAGEL, S. S. (1973) "Comparing Elected and Appointed Judicial Systems." Sage Professional Papers in American Politics, 1, 04-001. Beverly Hills, and London: Sage Pubns.

OR

(2) Nagel, Stuart S. 1973. *Comparing Elected and Appointed Judicial Systems.* Sage Professional Papers in American Politics, vol. 1, series no. 04-001. Beverly Hills and London: Sage Publications.

CONTENTS

Introduction 5

PROBLEMS OF CONCEPTUALIZATION, EVIDENCE AND INFERENCE 9

Fulbright's Operational Code:
Philosophical Beliefs 20

> Nature of Politics 20
> Perception of Malignant Forces in World Politics 25
> Perception of Benign Forces in World Politics 33
> Optimism - Pessimism 37
> Predictability of the Future 41
> Control of Historical Development 43
> The Role of Chance 46

Fulbright's Operational Code:
Instrumental Beliefs 49

> Selecting Goals for Political Action 49
> Pursuit of Goals 58
> Calculation and Control of Risks 60
> Timing 63
> Role and Utility of Different Means 64

Conclusions 68

> Cross-Sectional Variability 70
> Longitudinal Variability 72

Notes 79

References 80

KURT K. TWERASER is Assistant Professor of Political Science at the University of Arkansas, Fayetteville. Within a larger research interest in international relations and foreign policy formation, he has for several years worked on aspects of decision-making, especially perceptual and cognitive processes in political leadership. Presently he is engaged in research on operational codes of Austrian political leaders of the interwar period, and a community power structure study of the city of Linz, Austria. He holds a Ph.D. in International Studies from The American University, Washington, D.C.

Changing Patterns of Political Beliefs: The Foreign Policy Operational Codes of J. William Fulbright, 1943-1967

KURT K. TWERASER
University of Arkansas

INTRODUCTION

It is generally acknowledged that a foreign policy decision maker is influenced by a variety of factors in making his calculations. Beliefs have been one of the variables presumed important to the study of decisional outputs. Yet presumed importance has not been matched by increased scholarly inquiry, largely due to the lack of adequate conceptual tools for dealing with the effects of beliefs on foreign policy calculations.

One promising tool for the study of political beliefs has been provided by Alexander George's (1969) reformulation of Nathan Leites' (1951, 1953) Bolshevik "operational code." The George construct (1969: 201-216) consists of five philosophical and five instrumental questions, answers to which will probably comprehend an actor's political beliefs.

Philosophical questions:

(1) What is the "essential nature" of political life? Is the political universe essentially one of harmony or conflict? What is the fundamental character of one's political opponents?

(2) What are the prospects for the eventual realization of one's fundamental political values and aspirations? Can one be optimistic or

---

AUTHOR'S NOTE: *An earlier version of this paper was presented at the Annual Meeting of the American Political Science Association, September 4-8, 1973, at New Orleans. In revising the original paper, the author owes a special debt to his graduate assistant, Gregory L. Diercks.*

must one be pessimistic on this score, and in what respect the one and/or the other?

(3) Is the political future predictable? In what sense and to what extent?

(4) How much "control" or "mastery" can one have over historical development?

(5) What is the role of "chance" in human affairs and in historical development?

Instrumental or policy questions:

(1) What is the best approach for selecting goals or objectives for political action?

(2) How are the goals of action pursued most effectively?

(3) How are the risks of political action calculated, controlled, and accepted?

(4) What is the best "timing" of action to advance one's interest?

(5) What is the utility and role of different means for advancing one's interest?

The task of the paper is to make explicit and systematic with the aid of the George construct two sets of beliefs guiding J. William Fulbright's work as a foreign policy legislator between 1943 and 1967. The first set consists of the rules the Senator believes to be instrumental for performance in foreign affairs, such as beliefs about the proper role of the legislature in the foreign policy process and his conceptions of the desirable national role for the United States. The second set of beliefs is of an epistemological nature—philosophical premises about life, politics, and international relations—which through their brooding presence, as it were, inform the more instrumental beliefs.[1]

Why is it important to discuss a legislator's operational code? Individual legislators, although not central foreign policy decision makers, can be viewed as "proximate" policymakers (Lindblom, 1968: 30-31) —close to the making of decision. How close, of course, depends on the issue, which in turn influences the size of the decision-making circle, the openness of the process, and the time allowed for deliberation. Consequently, the involvement of legislators in the executive-dominated foreign policy environment will vary with the above conditions. Fulbright qualifies as an important participant in the decision-ratifying process in American foreign policy. He has had considerable impact on the formation of public attitudes either in support of Presidential policies or in dissent against them. One of his fundamental strengths has been in the realm of education—his capacity to raise issues and thereby shape national opinion. While he was by no means solely responsible for the revolt against the Vietnam policy in 1967, he must be considered one of the prime movers. On this count alone, discussion of his code is appropriate.

Proximity of a legislator to decision-making is a function of his position in the hierarchy of his working environment, the U.S. Congress. Fulbright entered the House in 1943 as a Representative from Arkansas' Third District and served one term on the Foreign Affairs Committee. In 1944, he ran successfully for the Senate and has been the junior Senator from Arkansas ever since. His initial committee assignments in the Senate proved to be a source of frustration. Only the Banking and Currency Committee, which then had jurisdiction over foreign loans, provided an outlet for his international interests. Until 1949, he was denied Foreign Relations, the principal and most prestigious mouthpiece of the Senate in foreign affairs. Like others trying to lay the groundwork for the solution to long-range political problems, he was bound to be discouraged by a committee system that stands for marginal adjustments of existing policies rather than for major changes according to rationalist comprehensive plans (Morrow, 1969: 199).

One may generalize with Levi (1970) that the greater the distance of national leaders from the locus of foreign policy-making, the greater the opportunity to direct pronouncements on foreign affairs toward vague role conceptions for their nation rather than specific choices of intermediate objectives and means. It is thus not accidental that the operational code of legislators will be long on philosophical and short on instrumental items. At the same time, it is reasonably clear that the general vagueness of foreign policy pronouncements of persons distant from the point of leverage in foreign policy making is not a function of their lack of intelligence, perspicacity, and political know-how. This is borne out by their different behavior in situations where they are directly responsible (Huitt, 1954: 340-365). Fulbright has been a resourceful practitioner of the legislative game, and a skillful provider for his constituency's well-being and for his own political survival.

The time span covered by Fulbright's career coincides with two major adaptations of United States foreign policy—the creation and the breakdown of the cold war foreign policy consensus. Starting out as a champion of international government, he had to adjust by 1946 to the failure of the United Nations to secure global peace. World order based on the frontiers of 1945 and guaranteed by close U.S.-Soviet cooperation did not materialize. Instead, it seemed that the main threat to peace was Communist expansion, to be countered by a network of regional organizations which would make up for the weakness of the global organization. In the middle 1960s, it was Vietnam that forced Fulbright into yet another major re-examination and realignment of his beliefs on international politics.

Analysis of Fulbright's operational code begins in 1943, the year he entered Congress. The cut-off year, 1967, must appear arbitrary to the reader. However, since the purpose of the investigation was to shed light on operational code change, the cut-off point appeared legitimate as soon as it was reasonably clear that the new operational code adopted towards the end of 1965 was not ephemeral but had staying power. By analyzing a somewhat remote period, better control could be exercised over the ever-present danger of investigator bias intruding into the analysis.

A further advantage of studying legislators lies precisely in their not being central policy makers. Analysis of one of the "lesser" figures in policy making minimizes the temptation to look for pathological and/or idiosyncratic behavior generally associated with the charismatic leader. As Glad has suggested (1973: 309), it is easier to generalize from the beliefs of moderately successful leaders who reflect contemporary ideas in their belief systems with relative clarity.

Finally, the question arises: why explain Fulbright in terms of cognitive rather than psychodynamic and psychogenetic variables? Why study beliefs and not character? One could argue that Fulbright's personal political successes in his early legislative career—the Fulbright Resolution, his victory in his bid for the Senate, and the Fulbright Exchange Act—established patterns of thought and behavior upon which he was tempted to fall back in later crises. These early successes propelled him from relative obscurity to national attention and infused him with the type of confidence necessary for further success. It was during these years that he developed his own style. According to Barber (1968: 52), style can be viewed as a bundle of strategies for adapting, for protecting and enhancing self-esteem. The style's staying power, Barber hypothesized further (1968: 78), may derive from a solution to the Eriksonian identity crisis. The manifest signs, that is, the style, may refer to much deeper developments in the subject's character. But as George (1974: 264) has pointed out, "it is risky to infer from the presence of traits at the phenomenological layer of behavior that a deep-seated personality need exists for that kind of behavior." The nature of the evidence available for analyzing Fulbright was better suited to describe phenomenological characteristics than to establish personality dynamics or identify even deeper-seated developmental experiences. It was difficult enough to infer operational code items from verbal behavior.

PROBLEMS OF CONCEPTUALIZATION, EVIDENCE AND INFERENCE

Underlying the "operational code" approach is the assumption that, since facts rarely "speak for themselves," decision makers must make sense out of an immensely confusing and noisy "reality" by using pre-existing sets of beliefs to assimilate new information (Axelrod, 1973: 1248-1266).

Given the human limitations of decision-making—the fragmentary nature of information available, the delay in its transmission, and the difficulties of correct storage and retrieval—"bounded" rather than perfect rationality, "satisficing" rather than maximizing behavior is to be expected.[2]

The interdependence of hypotheses and facts is both necessary and dangerous—necessary because facts take on meaning only within the context of a theory; dangerous because rigidities introduced by these hypotheses may hinder the detection and correction of error.[3] To explain and predict an actor's behavior we must understand the way in which his necessarily simplified model of reality is constructed. The building stones of the model are what Herbert Simon (1957a: 79) has called decision premises.

The "operational code" is probably best understood as the belief portions of the decisional premises, emphasizing the rational factors in human behavior rather than the affective, nonrational, or irrational ones (Simon, 1957b: 200-201). This seems close to George's (1969: 199) use of the term "operational code" as an "interrelated set of beliefs about the nature of political strategy and tactics." In another context, George (1972: 768) pointedly differentiates between ideological values, "operational code" beliefs, and other cognitive beliefs. De-emphasis of irrational factors is also evident in Robert Jervis' (1968, 1972) treatment of perception and in Sidney Verba's (1961) assessment of the degree to which foreign policy decision-making is grounded in rational processes.

Unfortunately, distinctions between the belief and affective aspects of cognitions are fuzzy, although these distinctions appear to be vital from the standpoint of vigorous analysis of how and why decisions are made. The operational indices of the belief aspects of cognitions are primarily the categories "true" and "false," "correct" and "incorrect," "probable" and "improbable," "likely" and "unlikely," "existent" and "non-existent;" the indices for attitudes refer primarily to "good" and "bad," "harmful" and "beneficial," "wise" and "foolish," "sick" and "healthy."[4] However, some political analysts subsume beliefs under attitudes and, what is worse, begin to fuse what is real and possible with what is good and bad. But clearly, while we tend to believe what we like and disbelieve what we dislike, there is no necessary correlation. A belief can change without a corresponding change in attitude. Also, political actors may differ in belief but have similar attitudes, or vice versa. Carelessness in differentiating between beliefs and attitudes may result in misinterpretation of an actor's behavior. It may, for example, be more important to know how a political actor believes foreign policy is made than whether he likes or dislikes the policy and yet is unwilling to do something about it.

This is, of course, not to argue that existential propositions expressing what human beings consider to be facts are not intimately linked with evaluative postulates. Thus, the belief that the future is predictable will enhance the value of the predictive enterprise (Brim, et al., 1962: 55). We contend that conceptual clarity might go far in making the "operational code" a more effective tool of explanation, and we therefore suggest restricting the construct to beliefs. Attitudes or valences are derived from the belief context, but not necessarily in a "psychological" manner, although there may be instances in which beliefs themselves may be structured in an illogical way.

Examples for conceptual fusion abound. J. David Singer (1968) conceives of attitudes as the individual's perceptions of the way things *are* done in his "life space," his preferences for the way things *should* be done, and his predictions as to the way things probably *will* be done (emphasis in original). The same author (1964: 425) defines the foreign policy operational code as a set of assumptions, expectations, and *preferences* (emphasis added). Relatively free of the tendency to fuse value, attitude and belief is Ole Holsti's (1970) treatment of John Foster Dulles' operational code. A narrow probabilistic conception of "operational code" is also apparent in Robert Jervis' (1970: 12) definition of it as "beliefs about what behavior will lead actors, or classes of actors to respond in specified ways." Ronald Stupak (1969: xix, 114) conceives of the operational code in his study of Dean Acheson as "those rules that Acheson believes to be essential for the effective performance of the Secretary of State in his role as policy-maker," together with the philosophical perceptions of the Secretary of State on life, politics, and international relations.

More troublesome is Sidney Verba's (1965: 516) use of beliefs in his definition of political culture as a system of beliefs about patterns of political interaction and political institutions. Beliefs refer not only to the cognitive aspects of thought, but to evaluative and expressive aspects as well. David S. McLellan (1971: 52) explicitly speaks of Dean Acheson's "philosophic beliefs and attitudes." Robert D. Putnam (1971: 651) subsumes politically relevant beliefs, values, and habits of the leaders of a political system under the term "attitude." In a discussion of restraints on overt American military intervention, Herbert K. Tillema (1973: 33) includes the "operational code" of decision makers, defining it as perception of threat and moral acceptability (or "attitudes on the morality of using force"). K. J. Holsti (1972: 369) lists attitudes, values, beliefs, ideologies, and analogies under the "operational code" construct. The height of comprehensive usage is reached by Richard J. Barnet (1971) in his work on the operational code of the national security managers. Other suggestive treatments of political actors utilizing the George construct have been produced by Dennis Kavanagh (1971) on Ramsey MacDonald, D. Gordon White (1970) on Mao Tse-Tung and Liu Shao-Ch'i, Ned Ashby (1970) on Schumacher and Brandt, G. G. Gutierrez (1973) on Dean Rusk, Loch Johnson (1973) on Frank Church, and Joel Anderson (1973) on Arthur Vandenberg.

It is obvious that unless we attend carefully to the boundary problem, there is some danger that the operational code construct will suffer the fate of the concepts of "ideology" and "belief system," meaning all things to all men.[5]

How does one tap the beliefs of decision makers? The simplest assumption would be: Actor X believes, therefore, he acts. However, the relationship between belief and action is rarely, if ever, one-to-one. Furthermore, when a political system does not demand from its leaders a coherently developed set of beliefs, one may very well encounter complete silence on beliefs particularly interesting to the investigator. The fact that beliefs and premises are not articulated in a systematic fashion does not necessarily mean that they are non-existent. But it does mean that considerable inferential leaps are necessary to bring them into the open.

The analyst may infer beliefs from the general behavior in a society, the behavior of subcultures, general foreign policy programs and objectives, the specific working environment of the subject, and his voting and verbal behavior. Reliance upon inference of this sort leaves much room for judgment and interpretation and, consequently, inaccuracy. The literature concerning the question of our assurance that an individual's verbal statements are a reliable indicator of overt behavior was reviewed recently with devastating results. In 32 studies reviewed, Wicker (1969) found little or no predictable relationship between attitudes and overt behavior. The article dealt with attitudes rather than beliefs, but it is not unreasonable to assume that beliefs may also be unrelated to behavior.

More generally, the observational field of the social scientist forces one to deal with abstractions or concepts at least one step removed from first-order data. Kalleberg (1969: 32) remarked:

> social reality has a specific meaning and relevance structure for the human living, acting, and thinking therein. Thus, the constructs of the social scientist are, so to speak, constructs made by the actors on the social scene, whose behavior the social scientist has to observe and explain in accordance with the procedural rules of his science.

Since as soon as one starts to speak or write, something is left out, writing from someone else's writing is at least two steps removed from hard data. Probably the only way to overcome these inferential hurdles is to immerse oneself in the totality of the data before one attempts to understand properly any portion of them. The ability to use data intelligently is, therefore, heavily dependent on the researcher's overall knowledge in the field to which the material is relevant.

What are the sources of J. W. Fulbright's beliefs? The primary data are public statements by the Senator, particularly those made "for the record," under the assumption that much of the Senatorial behavior that counts is public behavior. All of Fulbright's speeches in the U. S. *Congressional Record*, Vols. LXXXIX-CXIII, 1943-1967, were analyzed. In order to overcome certain evidential weaknesses of the Congressional Record as a documentation of the legislative process (Mantel, 1959), 60 hearings of the Senate Foreign Relations Committee from 1949 to 1967 were scrutinized, together with speeches delivered by Fulbright in a variety of non-Congressional environments and articles and books written by the Senator himself. The Senator has also given numerous interviews on television and to journalists; these have been used in their published versions. The author has also had access to the James William Fulbright Papers at the University of Arkansas Library, containing public correspondence and general legislative material for the years 1943 to 1960.[6] Fulbright's letters provided significant insights into his operational code. As Dexter (1956) pointed out, the writing of letters may be one of the most significant outlets and hence one of the more important bits of evidence for the researcher, especially when a letter is addressed to someone who has no axe to grind with respect to a particular issue.

The methodological criticism might be raised that relying predominantly on public statements will tend to shut out what a politician "really" believes. With Rosenau (1959: 343), one might answer that "it is the verbal behavior of Senators, and not what they 'really' think, that has consequences for the conduct and formulation of foreign policy." Huitt (1969: 162) also stresses the possibility of making valid, if crude, inferences about the rules for behavior from the printed record. He actually tested the assumption empirically in his study of the Morse Committee assignment controversy of 1952. First, he studied the incident wholly from the printed record. After that, he interviewed persons who had first-hand participant knowledge of the controversy. He concluded that, while it was possible to make some refinements, the conclusions did not have to be altered as a result of the interviews.

While one would wish to have hard indices rather than vague signals available to establish the beliefs of actors, the analyst must learn to make the best of imperfect data. Still, the problem of validity is genuine and whether inference is made from actual behavior or from what actors say, it will always be a formidable task to infer beliefs or, more precisely, the operational items of beliefs from language. Beliefs in principle will not do, since they do not give shape to indeterminate situations. The inferential task is to come up with the beliefs that do in fact determine actions and reactions of an actor when confronted by certain situations and issues.

It is a well-established fact that the audience has impact on the content of communication and that actors respond differently to different audiences. How this changes the content of beliefs has to be taken into account when making inferences. Some empirical evidence is available through a quantitative content analysis (Downs, 1963) of 24 speeches delivered by Fulbright on foreign affairs between February, 1959, and April, 1962. Not surprisingly, Fulbright stressed different themes before different audiences. There is, of course, no reason why the researcher cannot control for the impact of different audiences upon the speaker and take into account how his attempt to use communication for political purposes might have affected his public references and allusions. In additon to audience impact upon the actor and his "tailoring" of remarks to the particular communications medium being used, the analyst must also control for what might be called the temper of the times, that is, salient event features of the environment. The dangers of misinterpretation may be reduced by relying upon multiple sources of evidence rather than upon statements produced before one type of audience only.

The ancient human quirk of confusing beliefs in principle with beliefs in fact is in all likelihood less pronounced in political actors. Since politicians are concerned with influencing the behavior of many audiences, they are probably constrained, in order to make their communication tasks more manageable, to reduce the differences between private and public communications. The very redundancy of communications may actually be to the advantage of the researcher if one assumes that redundancy makes for reliability. One virtue of redundancy consists in removing the temptation to use every piece of evidence in reconstructing beliefs because of the very shortage of evidence. At the same time, redundancy should not be equated with a simple frequency count, since, to paraphrase George (1959b: 32), many individual inferences do not make a frequency indicator of a nonfrequency indicator. The inference is based on the presence of the belief, not the frequency of its occurrence, within each individual communication.[7]

Some important bits of evidence would simply not be registered in a purely quantitative analysis, since behaviors that occur infrequently have a way of escaping the sampling net. For example, this investigation started out with the generally accepted image of the contrast between Senator Fulbright, the moderate on the Cold War, and Secretary of State John Foster Dulles, the Cold Warrior incarnate. Perusal of hearings and the Congressional Record for the 1950s gradually convinced the investigator that the distance between Fulbright and Dulles on American foreign policy ends during the Cold War was exaggerated. And yet, a recent Guttman scaling of Senatorial attitudes during the Cold War (Stassen, 1972) established that Fulbright was a moderate on the Cold War as early as 1952. The discovery of a couple of isolated newspaper items, which would have been missed by quantitative methods, solved the puzzle. One was a 1951 Fulbright statement advocating massive retaliation, the other a 1954 statement advocating the sending of American ground troops to Indochina (Arkansas Gazette, 1951a; 1954). Both supported the hunch that the much-publicized Dulles-Fulbright clashes of 1957 were differences over means rather than ends.

Suffice it to say that the procedures employed were in consonance with the canons of history, among them special attention to primary sources and reliance upon secondary sources only when absolutely necessary. Still, reliance upon a qualitative rather than a quantitative approach does raise the question of reliability. What assurance is there that another investigator will arrive at similar interpretations of the historical data?

A partial test of coder reliability is available through a presently ongoing evaluative assertion analysis by the author and a collaborator (M. Glenn Newkirk, Ph.D. candidate, GSIS, Univ. of Denver). We analyze Fulbright's beliefs about U.S. and U.S.S.R. capabilities and foreign policy successes and failures and their correlations with his perception of friendship and hostility of the two countries. We assume that the friendship-hostility perceptions tap what is one of the most important dimensions of the operational code, the image of the enemy. The following scores were established by the collaborator through an analysis of all of Fulbright's statements pertaining to the Soviet Union in the Congressional Record every third year between 1943-1967. The values of the statements, after translation into standardized sentence structures (see North et al., 1963) ranged from +3 (Soviet Union friendly) to -3 (Soviet Union hostile). The quantitative results bear out the judgments on Fulbright's image of the enemy.

TABLE 1

FULBRIGHT'S PERCEPTION OF THE SOVIET UNION

PERIOD	FRIENDSHIP/HOSTILITY SCORE
1943	+1.81
1946	-1.00
1949	-2.83
1952	-2.48
1955	-2.00
1958	-1.66
1961	-1.99
1964	-2.3
1967	+0.81

Cross-Sectional and Longitudinal Variability of the Operational Code

It is only against the background of continuity that a discussion of change makes sense. Fulbright appears to be a pragmatist in his approach to politics in general (Johnson and Gwertzman, 1968), and an internationalist in foreign affairs (Tweraser, 1971). How, then, can we explain (a) differences between Fulbright the foreign policy legislator, the politico in domestic politics, and the supporter of segregation in race politics; and (b) the differences between Fulbright, the utopian internationalist of 1945, the Cold Warrior of 1946-1963, and the dissenter of 1966? An attempt will be made to explain cross-sectional variability by discussing Fulbright's role conceptions, his cognitive styles, his decision-making models, and the nature of his commitments to institutions in various issue areas under the first philosophical item of the George construct, the nature of politics. The question of Fulbright's internationalism will be clarified through delineation of his conceptions of U.S. foreign policy roles under the first instrumental belief item, the selection of goals for political action.

Legislators are forced by the very nature of their profession to deal efficiently with a number of issue areas. Each issue area can be conceived of as a psychological environment activating different cognitive styles, different self-images, different models of representation, different models of decision-making, and different manners of commitment to institutions. Clausen (1973) has convincingly demonstrated that legislators make decisions by adjusting their decision rules (whether to act according to the wishes of the President, or in line with the party majority, or according to their own conscience) to the policy dimension to which they believe a particular issue belongs. While he differentiates five dimensions (government management, social welfare, agricultural assistance, international involvement, civil liberties), we adopted a simplified trichotomous construct consisting of a foreign policy issue area, our main interest; the race issue area, for contrast purposes; and other domestic issues, collapsed into a residual issue area, public welfare. How do various possible cognitive strategies and styles fit with the three issue areas?

As for cognitive strategies, it has been acknowledged (Glenn, 1966) that different types of situations call for different cognitive responses. Problems may be moderately difficult, in which case a strategy of "case-particularism" might be appropriate, requiring a two-step approach of hypothesis and verification. The first, abstract step determines the part of existing techniques which remain pertinent, and the second, empirical step adapts strategy to the peculiarity of the situation. There are difficult, but not unthinkable problems, and strategy resembles a universalistic model in which general ideas count and the expounder of the model displays little interest in persevering down to the level of detail. According to Glenn (1966: 131), the United States exhibits strong universalistic tendencies in foreign affairs, and operational codes have a programmatic character based on beliefs in certain universal panaceas. The latter strategy is very similar to Putnam's (1971: 661) "ideological style," described as a clustering of four primary characteristics: a consistent tendency to generalize, use abstract deductive theory, use specifically ideological terms, and refer to more ideal future states of society. It is also plausible that some problems may be judged to be insoluble, in which case they are better left alone. The appropriate cognitive style is one of "traditionalism" (Putnam, 1971: 662), the issue discussion being embedded in a historical context.

Closely related to cognitive styles are decision-making models. As Allison demonstrates (1971), decision makers in foreign policy tend to analyze their problems in terms of a rational actor model with unitary governments responding to threats and opportunities in the international system by choosing goals and objectives, designing a spectrum of options, deliberating on the consequences of each alternative, and selecting alternatives that maximize goals and objectives. An alternative model, accepted by most decision makers as the norm in domestic politics but as improper in foreign policy, is the bureaucratic politics paradigm (Allison, 1971; Allison and Halperin, 1972), where the interplay of parochial priorities and perceptions of various players and agencies make governmental action not a rational choice but the result of bargaining. One can also imagine a "no politics" model in certain issue areas where benign inactivity of the government is deemed appropriate.

Legislators must adopt models of representation of constituency interests, ranging from trustee to politico to instructed delegate (Wahlke et al., 1962). The various models reflect different beliefs about social distance—that is, the proper status relationship between representative and represented in different issue areas (Eulau, 1967). Legislators manage to eliminate role strains by assigning vastly different status to their constituencies depending on the nature of the issue area. In one issue area they may subordinate themselves entirely to their constituency as instructed delegates, in other areas they may believe in superior status for themselves, in still others they may strike a bargain between trustee and delegate tending towards the role of politico.

The manner of individual integration into systems may also vary from issue area to issue area. Integration may be achieved through ideological commitment to institutions. According to Kelman (1969), ideological integration on the part of a pragmatist implies a highly conditional form of support for the system, it being expected to evolve new institutions and approaches in the light of changing circumstances. At the other extreme, integration might be purely normative, based on a commitment to the system by virtue of unquestioning adherence to the rules reflecting a primary concern with preserving law and order. In between falls what Kelman calls role participant integration, a commitment to various social roles mediated by the system.

Intuitively, we may distribute the various models as indicated in Table 2. The schema lacks empirical validation and we cannot exclude the possibility that it may reflect the analyst's judgments

TABLE 2

MODES OF REALITY PROCESSING AND POLICY DIMENSIONS

MODES OF COGNITIVE ACTIVITY	ISSUE AREA FOREIGN POLICY	ISSUE AREA PUBLIC WELFARE	ISSUE AREA RACE
1. Cognitive Style	Universalistic	Partisan Pluralism	Traditional
2. Decision-Making Model	Rational Actor	Bureaucratic	Benign Inactivity
3. Representation of Constituency	Trusteeship	Politico	Instructed Delegate
4. Integration into System	Ideological	Role Participant	Normative

rather than the actor's approach. The trichotomy does injustice to the richness of empirical reality which probably is better caught through the use of continua on which actors can be plotted. The schema has been formulated in part via induction from the author's (1971) previous study of Fulbright. Therefore, circularity may be present. Still, the assumption that the various approaches to reality within each issue area are mutually linked is of considerable heuristic value. At least some features of the operational code display a cross-sectional variability within the same person, and a tentative explanation of this variability can be given in terms of issue contexts. Within each issue context we ought to expect persistence of cognitive style clusters for a long period of time, but how the nature of politics is perceived in, let us say, issue area "foreign policy" differs from perception in issue area "race."

Regarding the longitudinal variability of Fulbright's operational code, the problem was largely definitional. Two terms generally used to describe orientations towards foreign affairs are "isolationism" and "internationalism." However, when used in dichotomous form, they create the impression that foreign policy postures are inherently dualistic. They are thus unsuited to convey the diversity of political expression in a pluralist universe such as the United States (McFarland, 1969). It is methodologically more rewarding to think of isolationism and internationalism as two poles of a continuum ranging from total isolation to full involvement in global affairs.

Since Fulbright has been an internationalist throughout his career, the term does not explain variations. Obviously, additional dimensions must be introduced. It is here that the operational code can perform a useful function in reducing the undifferentiatedness of isolationism and internationalism. Since a policy maker's confidence in the destiny and influence of the United States has an important bearing on what type of involvement stance he advocates for his nation, the dimensions of the operational code dealing with optimism-pessimism, predictability of the future, and control of historical development will qualify advocacy. An optimistic capability judgment may lead those who are dissatisfied with the system into unrealistic demands for radical change; pessimistic estimates may induce passivity in world affairs. Theoretically, involvement stances range from assertion of absolute national sovereignty to collective defense arrangements to collective security to world government. The major questions will be whether the nation-state should retain complete control over its international security activities, whether control should be shared with alliance partners regionally, or whether the community of nations in the form of a global organization should exercise an ever-increasing control over them. As long as capability judgments are optimistic, internationalism may be "community-oriented" reformist leadership, or United States-controlled internationalism, either of the unilateral or multilateral variety. Isolationism, as long as optimism prevails, shows itself in an extreme variant of United States control through unilateral intervention and withdrawal. The direction of internationalism (international community-oriented or United States-controlled) will in turn depend on the image of the predominant enemy—the nation-state system itself, or a particular nation-state or group of nation-states.

Out of the subtle interplay of threat perception, capability judgments, and direction of international involvement emerge national role conceptions such as reformist leader, world policeman, leader of the free world, defender of the faith.[8] National role conceptions in turn will influence the major ends and means and capability judgments. From the preceding it should be clear that change in an operational code cannot simply be summarized by the terms internationalism and isolationism.

FULBRIGHT'S OPERATIONAL CODE: PHILOSOPHICAL BELIEFS

THE NATURE OF POLITICS

Belief 1: There is Nothing Very Rational About Politics, Internal or External. It is Usually Dominated by Emotions and Irrational Procedures.

Belief 2: Politics is Man's Attempt to Inject Rationality Into a Conflictful But Ultimately Manageable Universe.

Belief 3: Domestic Policy is Based on Bargaining.

Belief 4: Foreign Policy Must Be Based On Rational Choice.

Belief 5: The Best Governmental Policy is No Policy.

Fulbright believes that people are usually moved by irrational forces. He attributes this pernicious phenomenon of irrationality to human nature. It is a product of biological heritage in which man's aggressive instincts are stronger than man's desire for peace (1967a), and, as if this were not enough of a predicament, irrationality is also a product of man's aggressive habits (1969a: 145). This rather pessimistic view of human nature is balanced by the belief that man is also endowed with reason, which may help him to acknowledge his animal inheritance and thereby control it (1966b: 161). Certainly, the very fact that Fulbright has remained in politics since 1943 is a powerful indicator that he believes human beings are endowed with some capability for choice. We might say that history consists for Fulbright of man's endeavor to control irrationality through organized efforts on the part of government and people, although he often complains that "there is nothing very rational about politics, internal or external" (Senate Committee on Foreign Relations, 1960: 213).

As President of the University of Arkansas (1939-1941), Fulbright vigorously asserted that manifestations of irrationality had to be tackled in a rational manner. Arkansas' developmental imbalance, plagued as the state was by outside economic domination, internal corruption, and poverty, could be rectified by a dose of rationality in the form of education and political leadership. History, even Arkansas history, was not made by large interests and organizations alone. The individual, properly educated and wisely led, would overcome the confining conditions of underdevelopment (1939).

In national domestic politics, abuses of power could be counteracted by education and traditions which check the perennial struggle for influence between the branches of government (1951a: 448); but in foreign policy, the constitutional arrangements for political adjustment were clearly inadequate "in a world that obstinately refuses to conduct its affairs under Anglo-Saxon rules of measured and orderly procedures" (1961a: 2). Rationality could not be brought to bear upon international affairs through a system in which power and responsibility for foreign policy were shared and overlapping and thus unable to produce unified policies oriented to a clear and definite conception of national purpose.

Even more somber was the note he struck in commenting on the race question in the South (U.S. Congress, 1958a: 19852-19853).

> History tells us that race memories long endure. They are sentimental and emotional, and when stirred up, they become irrational. . . . Bearing in mind that flesh and blood is weak and frail, these problems might yield to the slow conversion of the human heart rather than to the remedies of a more emergent nature.

It is a constant in human affairs that whenever social convictions are profoundly violated, human beings are "likely to react almost by involuntary reflex and often violently" (U.S. Congress, 1958a: 19852-19853).

An insecure person would probably falter under the impact of these contradictions, but politicians are made of sturdy stuff. Fulbright, like other legislators, solved the question of the proper mix between what he conceived to be the demands for efficiency in government and public accountability by developing a self-image which enabled him to develop different operational codes for different issue areas. In dealing with the question of whether a representative must do what his constituents want, or what he thinks best, he was acutely aware of the ambiguities attached to legislative work and was able to define for himself relationships to his constituents, to the nation, and to his own conscience that remained fairly stable throughout his career (U.S. Congress, 1946a: A1284-1286; 1963a; 1968a: 64-65).

In the race question, Fulbright was aware that expectations of the constituency might go so overwhelmingly in one direction that independent action would be self-defeating (U.S. Congress, 1946a: A1284; 1966a: 64). Isolationism was singled out as the issue worth risking his career over; "regardless of how strongly opposed my constituents may prove to be to the creation of, and participation in, an ever stronger United Nations organization, I would follow such a policy in that field unless it becomes clearly hopeless" (U.S. Congress, 1946a: A1284).

In his self-image, then, Senator Fulbright appeared to adopt diametrically opposed conceptions of representation for two important issue areas: the instructed-delegate model for civil rights, submitting entirely to popular mandate; and a model for foreign policy-making close to the concept of representation generally associated with Edmund Burke, refusing to serve the constituency's will though not its interest. Foreign policy was an issue area which must be subject to the rational deliberation of wise statesmen, the superior wisdom presumably either residing in himself or the executive branch (1963a; 1964a: 46). On the other hand, in civil rights, Fulbright did not claim (either for himself or the national government) any superior judgment and believed in humoring the opinions of the people.

A violation of what he believed the proper status relationship in civil rights was apt to trigger rather vigorous responses accusing those who upset that relationship of the vice of intellectual arrogance. In answer to an article praising Fulbright as a true liberal because of his independence, the Senator found himself, not unexpectedly, in complete agreement and he mused (1950a):

> I have often thought how paradoxical it is that men like Humphrey are called liberal when in fact they are the most intolerant and dictatorial members of the Senate. They . . . know all of the answers to all of the problems and are quite willing to use all of the forces at their command to compel obedience to their will.

In the public welfare dimension, Fulbright's model of representation was that of the politico striking bargains between the national Democratic party and his constituency interests. Fulbright has been a good provider for Arkansas, craftily using the opportunities open to a resourceful politician in an incremental decision-making process. It would be hard to pin any ideological label on him in this issue-area—conservative liberal would do just as well as liberal conservative—apart from a cautious belief in the beneficial function of government in producing public good.

It is interesting to note that different styles of reasoning go together with different models of representation in various issue contexts. This variability is, of course, most pronounced in the two areas furthest removed in terms of the degree of governmental centralization Fulbright believed appropriate. In civil rights, the delegate model was matched by a philosophical stance of traditionalism—references to the South and to the Southern mind abound. Occasionally, the South assumes the form of a past utopia—almost a paradise lost—providing a standard to judge adversely certain developments engendered by modernization, urbanization, and industrialization (1953-54: 65-66). The race issue is invariably placed in a historical-philosophical context, the judgment on human nature is extremely pessimistic, the issue is not believed susceptible to political solution but must be left to the healing influence of time, education, and the slow conversion of the human heart (U.S. Congress, 1958b: 19853-19853). The criterion for government policy is social acceptability. Consequently, the most effective policy is no policy.

In foreign policy, the representational model of trusteeship was associated with a pronounced universalistic style. Fulbright's reasoning is heavily synoptic, analysis is deduced from general abstract models, less attention is given to the particulars of each case, parochial interests are rejected as possible criteria for judging policy, political acceptability of a policy is subordinated to efficiency, and ideal futures are occasionally invoked. His image of the proper institution to make foreign policy is clearly influenced by the rational actor model. Echoing Alexis de Tocqueville, Fulbright asserted that democracies were inherently at a disadvantage in foreign policy, since the only foreign policy a democracy could successfully engage in—an isolationist one—was no longer possible. Domestic acceptability narrowed the range of choices open to the Executive; coalition diplomacy tended to concentrate foreign affairs powers in the hands of the President and downgrade the role of Congress and the electorate. Due to the complexity of the subject matter, the age of the foreign policy amateur was over (U.S. Congress, 1959a: 6194-6195).

Fulbright compared the almost unmanageable American governmental machinery with what he believed to be the advantages of a monolithic authoritarian state, such as the Soviet Union, in foreign policy. Moreover, in the Soviet Union, the people who participated in the decision-making process had a very clear conception of their role in the world (U.S. Congress, 1959b: 6193-6194). In the United States system, in which power and responsibility for foreign policy were shared and overlapping, no unified policies could be devised. The workings of the sprawling administrative apparatus and the checks and balances of Congressional authority in foreign relations imposed serious restraints upon rational policy-making. Therefore, he believed that the price of democratic survival in a world of aggressive totalitarianism is to give up some of the democratic luxuries of the past, however distasteful and dangerous it may be to vest the Executive with powers unchecked and unbalanced (1961a: 5, 7). These beliefs are a perfect example of the hypothesis that "actors tend to see the behavior of others as more centralized, disciplined and coordinated than it is" (Jervis, 1968: 475).

It is only fair to add that Fulbright's beliefs changed after 1965 on issues of Presidential-Congressional relations, the role of public opinion, and even race. But it also seems fair to say that from his entry into politics in 1943 to the end of 1965, he did analyze "reality" with the help of the models mentioned, and he used different models in different issue areas.

Belief 6: The Survival of Civilization Depends Heavily Upon the Quality of Leadership.

As a teacher of government and law and as University President, Fulbright emphasized his belief in the importance of good government and urged students to consider politics as the most honorable of professions (Johnson and Gwertzman 1968: 28, 38). The election of good leaders, he believed, was the major function of the electorate, and he suggested that the legislature in a democracy is generally a reflection of the electorate (1946b: 7, 65-66). A corollary of the high trust he put in leadership was his belief in noblesse oblige and in a politics of civility. Those who were privileged had to turn to public service and had to display high standards of conduct. Personal integrity and a certain demeanor on the part of leaders were essentials of good government. Corruption in government undermined the moral strength of the people and was not just a matter of domestic affairs but had grave foreign policy implications.

"Without confidence in their government, the people will not make the sacrifices necessary to oppose Russia successfully," Fulbright asserted (U.S. Congress, 1951b: 2905). Drawing upon Toynbee's thesis that the majority of great civilizations had been destroyed as a consequence of domestic corruption rather than external aggression, he wondered whether:

> in recent years we have unwittingly come to accept the totalitarian concept that the end justifies the means, a concept which is fundamentally and completely antagonistic to a true democratic society. . . . Democracy is more likely to be destroyed by the perversion of, or abandonment of, its true moral principles than of armed attack from Russia. The evil and invidious materialism of the Communists is a greater danger to us than their guns.

Fulbright is fairly close to Dulles' concepts of moral law and moral power (Guhin, 1972: 116-128). He is also caught in the familiar circularity of democratic foreign policy theory where the people are the source of policy and at the same time, because of their ignorance of foreign affairs, must be prevented from interfering in foreign policymaking.

PERCEPTION OF MALIGNANT FORCES IN WORLD POLITICS

Belief 7: The Enemy is National Sovereignty.

This belief of Fulbright's possessed amazing continuity although we can discern shifts of emphasis in his advocacy of the best means to do away with the principle of self-help in international politics. Initially, sovereignty was to be curtailed by a delegation of certain security functions to an international organization which would eventually become a world government. When this approach became hopeless, sovereignty was to be attacked at the regional level, especially in Western Europe. Increasingly, sovereignty also became the long-range target of functionalism and education.

Fulbright was extremely dissatisfied with the rules of the game and the pattern of authority characterizing the nation-state system. During the early phase of his legislative career (1943-1945), Fulbright believed that the United States must pursue a foreign policy which would progressively enable the community of nations to control the security destiny of its members. The transfiguration of the balance of power into world government was to be a gradual process, based upon cooperation between the great powers. Fulbright's belief in structural reform of the international system found legislative expression in the Fulbright Resolution, which put the House of Representatives on record in favor of some form of postwar international collaboration. The innocuous wording of the resolution was a testimony to Fulbright's political astuteness and belied the beliefs underlying his approach to international politics at that time. He was not only thinking in terms of some tame international organization but clearly envisaged one equipped with a world police force, and he also believed in the necessity of controlling the very capacity of nations to produce instruments of war (U.S. Congress, 1943a: A2398; and 1945a: A3624).

In consonance with his anti-nationalist model of international politics, he believed the central feature of the Dumbarton Oaks proposal, the principle of sovereign equality of all peace-loving states, was objectionable because the future international organization might undertake to preserve for all time every member state as it presently existed. The organization should not be the instrument of reaction nor the means of freezing the status quo forever. On the contrary, it should be the means by which the development of the world could be orderly (U.S. Congress, 1945b: 2899).

For realists, like Dean Acheson, sovereignty was the original fact of the international system. For Fulbright, sovereignty was the original sin of international politics. Sovereignty resided in the people or community, not in the governments which they created, and "the people may delegate any powers they wish to their representatives but they do not delegate their sovereignty to their government." When a government no longer fulfills completely the purpose for which it was created, he pointed out (New Republic, 1945a: 158-159)

> it is entirely appropriate, in fact, it is essential that our people consider the delegation of power to some other and higher or-

ganization which is reasonably designed to perform the functions which this government cannot perform.

The corollary belief to the perniciousness of sovereignty was the belief that government and law were necessary to control the small, lawless minority who refuse to abide by the rules of society, whether national or international. In his peace-by-government phase, Fulbright conceived the international system as being in a Hobbesian state of nature and drew heavily upon the American experience to justify the use of force and the establishment of government (U.S. Congress, 1943b: A1180; and 1944a: A413).[9] This transposition of principles, rules, and procedures that have proved effective in a national system to the sphere of international politics is also apparent in Fulbright's belief that international law had to be compulsory if it was to be effective (U.S. Congress, 1945c: 8102, 8157). The danger that this approach might be counterproductive in terms of the amount of violence necessary to enforce international criminal law was mitigated by the stipulation that individuals rather than nations should be punished.

However, the cold war challenged Fulbright's assumption that the experience and categories of municipal law were applicable at a global level and inclined him to work to achieve redemption of history at the regional level. He had believed that Europe must be rebuilt in such a way as to transcend the nation-state. In the middle 1950s, Fulbright changed his belief about European unity; while still asserting that the United States "might well have exploited the opportunity provided by the European recovery program to push the hesitant European nations toward political federation," he realized that, rather than chasing after federalist chimera, processes had to be devised which were more attuned to the "real world of sovereign nation-states and diverse and hostile communities" (1961b : 13, 16). De Gaulle's veto of British entry into the Common Market reactivated the belief, for the Gaullist philosophy was "designed to restore and conserve the classical balance of power-system among sovereign nations . . . by adjusting it to the specifications of the age of super-states and nuclear weapons." The real culprit was still the nation-state, and Fulbright (1963b: 42, 45; and 1964a: 108) believed it imperative "to alter in the most fundamental manner the traditional sovereignty and self-determination."

By 1965, the dominant belief with respect to transcending the nation-state was that functionalist enterprises and education were the appropriate tools to circumvent antagonisms between East and West, between rich nations and poor nations. Man must recognize "that the nation performs its essential function not in its capacity as a *power*, but in its capacity as a *society* . . . that the primary business of the nation is not itself but its people" (Fulbright, 1966a: 256 and 1966d: 240). The problem of international community was no longer institutional but psychological:

> If there is any key to survival and security in the nuclear age, it lies not in new and improved international peacekeeping organizations, nor in elaborate schemes for disarmament and disengagement, but in the personal attitudes of nations and their leaders, in their willingness to place the common requirements of humanity over conflicting aspirations and ideologies [Fulbright, 1965c].

Belief 8: The Enemy is Soviet Aggressive Totalitarianism (1946-1963).

After initial vacillation, Fulbright believed Soviet intentions to be aggressive and, indeed, as late as 1964, no doubts were evident about who was responsible for the onset of the cold war—the Soviet Union—and about the appropriateness of the U.S. response—containment (1964a: 82). Initially, he was hesitant to turn away from the doctrine of American-Soviet collaboration, accusing the Truman administration of applying a double standard to actions of the United States and the U.S.S.R. (U.S. Congress, 1945d: 10963).

However, by May, 1946, Fulbright voiced public doubts as to the U.S.S.R.'s intentions. He saw in the Soviet response to the U.S. version of international atomic control a significant clue to answer the question, "Is it the purpose of Russia to dominate the world through a subtle combination of infiltration and force, or is she only seeking security?" While Fulbright believed that the United States should give generous consideration to legitimate Soviet security interests, he also believed that "a basic principle of our foreign policy must be that there is a point beyond which we cannot, in justice to ourselves and the civilization of which we are the heir, permit any nation to expand without offering resistance by force" (1946a: 48, 52).

By September, 1946, Fulbright was fully convinced of Soviet expansionism and the immoral nature of the Communist regime. Groping for an explanation of Soviet behavior, which he expected would continue to be aggressive, he found a ready-made analogy between Hitler's rule in Germany and Stalin's rule in Russia. What was common to both regimes was the violation of individual dignity.[10] It was time to study the writings of Lenin and Marx as blueprints of Communist pathology, for undoubtedly American foreign policy would have been much sounder in the 1930s "if we had absorbed and believed what Hitler said in *Mein Kampf*" (Northwest Arkansas Times, 1948a). The lesson was clear: no more Munichs. The model of totalitarian dictatorship which had served well to explain German and Japanese behavior was also useful to give meaning to Soviet moves in Eastern Europe, Iran, and the Far East. These moves, once fitted into Fulbright's cognitive structure, took on a destructionist character, indicative of a design to conquer the world (Northwest Arkansas Times, 1946a). Fulbright's strong belief is also indicated by his response to the contention of Secretary of Commerce Henry Wallace in 1946 that "we have no more business in the political affairs of Eastern Europe than Russia has in the political affairs of Latin America." For Fulbright, the great evil of Wallace's talk was "the accentuation of disunity within the United States and encouraging belief in Russia that the United States does not have a definite foreign policy" (Northwest Arkansas Times, 1946a). To Wallace's charge that aid to Greece was American imperialism, Fulbright responded that Wallace's speech sounded "just as though it had been written in the Kremlin" (Northwest Arkansas Times, 1947a).

Since there were no clear instances of Soviet physical attacks per se before Korea, the conclusion seems fair that it was perceived aggressive intent that brought about a change in Fulbright's image of the Soviet Union, and that perceived Soviet intent made sense in the light of a generic model of totalitarianism.(11)

Thus, from September, 1946, on, Fulbright consistently described Soviet foreign policy as a policy of aggressive totalitarianism and cited the opponent's unlimited goals as the major hindrance to accommodation. He did not reduce the cold war to a series of misunderstandings (Fulbright, 1963b: 20, 33).

How could the cold war come to an end? It was Fulbright's belief that if the West could maintain a reasonable balance of power, "the crusading spirit of the Russians may burn itself out in time . . . the Russians may tire of expanding their borders and turn their attention to internal matters" (Northwest Arkansas Times, 1946b). The West must try to induce the Soviet Union to pursue more moderate aims and use less dangerous methods. Under the protective umbrella of "situations of strength," diplomatic adjustment might become possible. Fulbright was very close to the realism of a Dean Acheson, but Fulbright and Acheson differed in their judgments of what the ultimate outcome of the cold war would be. Fulbright's underlying premise pointed to a qualitatively different international order, whereas Acheson tended to view the cold war as but another episode in a system of great-power politics. That system was no more likely to disappear after the cold war than after the two world wars (Stupak, 1969: 48-50).

Fulbright had no use, however, for the concept of "total victory" and was immune to the more pathological aspects of domestic anti-Communism. In his confrontations with General MacArthur and Senator Goldwater, he always stressed that it was Soviet aggressive imperialism, not Communism as such, that was the big issue in the cold war. It was the combination of Communism with the great military strength of Russia and the spillover of the totalitarian features of the Soviet system into its external behavior that concerned him (Senate Committee on Armed Services and Committee on Foreign Relations, 1951: 69-70, 138, 142, 298; U.S. Congress, 1961a: 13246-13247; 1963a: 13960-13962).

Belief 9: The Adversary Relationship of the United States with the U.S.S.R. is of a Limited Nature (1964 on).

The outcome of the Cuban missile crisis, realization of an almost complete rupture of relations between the Soviet Union and Communist China, and the signing of the partial nuclear test ban treaty were taken by Fulbright as indices of the changed adversary relationship with the U.S.S.R. (1964: 5, 61, 66). Fulbright's threat perception had changed. The Soviet Union had drawn back from extremely aggressive policies; both sides had implicitly repudiated a policy of "total victory," and the Soviet Union had acquiesced in American strategic superiority. Consequently, he believed in dealing with the Soviet Union as a great power, quite apart from the difference of ideology. He now viewed the goals of Marxism-Leninism as essentially symbolic language for the advancement of Soviet national interests. He was also alarmed about the deterioration of American domestic life brought about by the overemphasis on the cold war as a challenge to American moral principles rather than as a challenge to security (1964b).

The stark cognitive simplicity of the aggressor-defender model (Pruitt and Gahagan, 1972: 19) gave way to a more differentiated model of a mixed cooperative-conflict relationship between the United States and the U.S.S.R. The relationship was still analyzed as a competition between two rational actors, but greater cognitive complexity is apparent.

Belief 10: The Enemy is Asian Communism.

Fulbright's change in his images of the enemy did not yet touch the problem of Asia. He was convinced of the implacable hostility of China and of the necessity for opposing the expansion of Asian Communism, whether Chinese or North Vietnamese. Where Communism represented the status quo, as in Europe, Fulbright was for building bridges. Where he believed that Communism was intent upon changing the status quo, as in Asia, it had to be contained. Equipped with this premise, he took for granted the contrast between the peaceful Russians and the war-mongering Chinese—the Chinese being depicted as looking with equanimity on the vast casualties a nuclear war would cause (1964a: 57). Nothing could be gained from accommodation as long as the Peking regime maintained its attitude of implacable hostility toward the United States (1964a: 38).

With respect to Vietnam, Fulbright warned all Asian Communists in 1964 that "it should be clear to all concerned that the United States will continue to defend its vital interests." These vital interests presumably were "to establish viable, independent states in Indochina and elsewhere in Southeast Asia, which will be free and secure from the domination of Communist China and Communist North Vietnam . . . but not necessarily hostile to those regimes" (1964a: 43-44).

We may justifiably interpret these words as a vindication of the old American principle that change must come about peacefully. Fulbright had at that time no doubts about the fact of Vietnamese aggression, and his premise that Asian Communism was the implacable enemy made him a useful tool of President Johnson during the Gulf of Tonkin crisis. The incident "had to be understood both in terms of the immediate situation and in terms of the broader pattern of Communist military and subversive activities in southeast Asia over the past ten years" (U.S. Congress, 1964a: 18399). The "broader pattern of Communist activity" lent meaning to the incident, and also made him quite logically believe that the use of limited force was justified. This may be inferred from the warning he issued (U.S. Congress, 1964: 18400) to the Communist powers of Asia:

> They (North Vietnam and Communist China) can enjoy peace and security as long—but only as long—as they confine their ambitions within their own frontier. . . . their aggressive and expansionist ambitions, wherever advanced, will meet precisely that degree of American opposition which is necessary to frustrate them.

It was not until 1966 that Fulbright's image of Asian Communism changed. Underlying the image change were new perceptions of Chinese intentions—he now viewed that country as status-quo oriented; new perceptions of the indigenous participants in the conflict in Vietnam—he tended to view the conflict not as a case of North Vietnamese aggression but as a civil war; and new judgments on the efficacy of nationalism as more potent than Communism. The rationale of American intervention was transformed from vindication of the principles of collective security into imperialism.

Belief 11: The Enemy is the Arrogance of Power (1966 on).

By 1966, Fulbright (1966a: 9) detected in international politics "the tendency of great nations to equate power with virtue and major responsibilities with a universal mission." Identification of the "arrogance of power" as the enemy is intimately connected with Fulbright's reactions to the 1965 Americanization of the Vietnamese War and the intervention in the Dominican Republic. Up to this time, Fulbright's basic premise was that the United States was legitimately engaged in containing enemy expansionist goals in Asia. The experience of 1965 with U.S. foreign policy prompted Fulbright to revise his image of the Indochinese war. From the leadership of Western consolidationist actions against Communist expansionist actions, he saw the United States moving into the category of expansionist powers. He believed now that righteousness might lead to blindness about how one is perceived. While the United States regarded any Communist action as aggressive, it remained blind to the probability that American action might be interpreted as expansionist by the Communist powers. "Power tends to confuse itself with virtue . . . and a great nation is peculiarly susceptible to the idea that its power is a sign of God's favor, conferring upon it a special responsibility for other nations" (1966a: 3).

Therefore, what was required, he believed was "to think of the nation as more nearly a society than a power, as a political arrangement whose primary business was the regulation of internal rivalries and the advancement of the happiness of its citizens." If sovereignty is the enemy in structural terms, the arrogance of power is its corollary in perceptual terms (1966b). In a further move away from a black-and-white conception of international politics, Fulbright thus included the United States in his more differentiated image of the malignant forces rampant on the world stage. Within this framework, conflict lost its zero-sum game character, conflict resolution began to center increasingly on the discovery of mutual interests and the consequent creation of an atmosphere conducive to improved communication, increased trust, and extension of empathy to the adversary.

PERCEPTION OF BENIGN FORCES IN WORLD POLITICS

Belief 12: Tight Alliance Structures Under the Leadership of the United States Are a Fertile Field for the Redemption of History at the Regional Level (1946-1964).

Up to 1964, Fulbright was primarily Europe-oriented and conceived of relations between the United States and Europe in terms of both U.S. security interests and U.S. trusteeship of Western civilization. Initially, it was Fulbright's belief (1948a: 26, 13) that the United States must take the lead in reconstructing Europe on federal lines, since there would be no peace as long as Europe remained a "senseless conglomeration of separate economic and political entities." Thus, aid should be made contingent on the transplantation to the old shattered European world of the ideals of federalism which had brought the United States to its unique position. This he regarded as a preliminary step toward "our ultimate objective of a world of law to which all men are subject" (1948b: 153, 155). The respect the Truman administration showed to the sensibilities of the European sovereignties resulted in frequent clashes between Dean Acheson and Fulbright (Senate Committee on Foreign Relations, 1949a: 195-201). Underlying the arguments were undoubtedly the different beliefs they attached to the efficacy of the sovereign nation-state. Fulbright was the most extreme Senator in attempts to make Marshall Plan aid and the U.S. commitment under the North Atlantic Treaty dependent on a fixed schedule of accomplishment in the field of unification (Senate Committee on Foreign Relations, 1949b: Part 1, 252-254; Part 2, 369-370). Fulbright's beliefs on this matter are perhaps best caught in a letter to Allen Dulles (1948c):

> As a member of the Senate, I have told the representatives of the European countries that unless they make progress toward unification, I will not feel justified in continuing my support of the recovery program. Perhaps it should not be put this bluntly in public but the thought that we expect some constructive moves toward unification should be impressed upon them.

John Foster Dulles' positive approach to European unity was more to Fulbright's expectations. In fact, on this particular issue the two men were in complete agreement. Not unexpectedly, Fulbright (1953a) responded to Dulles' pressure upon the European countries to ratify EDC with the mild remark that "the reports of [Dulles'] demands . . . were very greatly exaggerated." After the defeat of EDC, Fulbright discovered supreme virtues in the neofunctionalist attempts at practical cooperation for the solution of specific European problems. Jean Monnet became the most authentic voice of new Europe for Fulbright (1962). Since a true European had to be a supranationalist, De Gaulle's concept of a "Europe of States" was anathema to Fulbright. De Gaulle's veto of British entry into the Common Market was answered by Fulbright (U.S. Congress, 1963b: 926) with the threat of an "agonizing reappraisal" of America's ability to contribute to European defense, which Fulbright believed was dependent upon a united and expanded Atlantic partnership.

Apparently, the Senator had difficulty conceiving of relations between the United States and European nations in nonhierarchical terms. His conception of equality among partners was perhaps most succinctly expressed in his counsel (1963b: 57) to European nations about the nature of the American commitment: "Our commitment to the defense of Europe is absolute and irrevocable . . . so long as the critical decisions that lead to war and peace are not removed beyond our influence and responsibility."

Belief 13: What is Needed Is a Period of Loosening Institutional Ties and Being Satisfied If Our Friends Create Pluralistic Security Communities (1965-).

In the shadow of Vietnam, a good many problems which had activated his beliefs about European unity in previous years became occasions for philosophical reflections on the ups and downs in history rather than for vigorous transatlantic conceptual exchanges. He believed now (1965a) that the Atlantic area had become a pluralistic security community. He even believed by 1966 (Senate Committee on Foreign Relations, 1966: 111) that it was "too simple to blame President De Gaulle for the problems that have arisen in our relations in Europe;" thus, he finally acknowledged that the failure of the Atlantic partnership to live up to his expectations was not primarily due to the foibles of De Gaulle but to the much deeper current of malaise in the fields of alliance and economic relationships between the United States and Europe.

[35]

A similar change in Fulbright's beliefs about the virtue of engagement took place with regard to U.S.-Latin American relations. While he was not particularly interested in Latin America, he believed for a long time (U.S. Congress, 1945e: 2025-2026; and 1959c: 13442) in the appropriateness of multilateral arrangements between the United States and Latin America. The Alliance for Progress was welcomed (U.S. Congress, 1961b: 11705), since "in Latin America, as in much of the rest of the world, the question is being posed: Can social and economic progress proceed apart from totalitarian discipline? It is our duty to provide a credible base for the affirmative side of the debate." However, the unilateral character of the United States' intervention in the Dominican Republic in April, 1965, convinced him (U.S. Congress, 1965a: 23861) that in view of the profound antipathy of Latin America towards the overpowering neighbor, the United States might best help Latin America by encouraging it to find its own way through

> a loosening of existing ties and institutional bonds . . . [and] in the creation of a situation in which Latin American countries would be free, and would feel free, to maintain or sever existing ties as they see fit . . . and establish new arrangements, both among themselves and with nations outside the hemisphere, in which the United States would not participate.

Belief 14: World Trade Makes for World Peace.

Believing strongly in the healing hand of commerce, Fulbright was a strong supporter of trade liberalization, improvement of investment climate, reconstruction of the European economies, investment guarantees, and, at an ever-increasing scale during the cold war, the provision of public capital through bilateral and multilateral institutions (Tweraser, 1971). He believed that a worldwide multilateral system of trade and payments must be restored and maintained with the help of international agreements. He praised the advantages accruing to the "greatest producing nation in the world" from the reasonably free and stable conditions in international trade brought about by the Bretton Woods Agreement (U.S. Congress, 1945f: 7672). Without the International Monetary Fund, the United States would find itself obliged to supply exports in the form of outright grants. If other countries were in no position to pay, obviously American exports could not increase; aid instead of trade would be the result. But increasing exports by extending dollar loans through multilateral institutions was only one aspect of Fulbright's concern with commerce. Establishing a worldwide trend toward free trade policy by lowering American tariffs was another. In the periodic extensions of the Reciprocal Trade Agreements Act, Fulbright's voice was clearly heard against the protectionist rumblings in the Senate. "What we are primarily concerned with is the preservation of a system of private trading among nations" (U.S. Congress, 1945g: 6254-6255). He apparently believed that the structure of exports and imports in a free trade system would be equitable enough to encourage each country to exercise its comparative advantages and thereby share in the rising prosperity of all.

The healing powers of commerce took on additional meaning in the fight against Communism. Since Communism thrived on economic stagnation, correction of the situation would curtail the threat. Whether with respect to the loan to Britain in 1946 or the Marshall Plan, he believed that the prosperity of the United States, and with it the prosperity of the world, required reversing the trend toward world socialism and this, in turn, required helping to sustain the nations that might be useful in preserving world stability. As he put it in a letter to the publisher of the Arkansas Democrat, August Engel (1945b):

> If we do not help the British commonwealth to maintain a system of trading between individuals, in a very few years the only international trade will be between governments, and I am positive that we would not profit under such a system. In addition to that, I believe such a system would materially contribute to the continuation of conditions which would bring on another war.

While Fulbright has become famous for his support of foreign aid up to 1963, it must be emphasized that the ideological underpinnings of his foreign aid concepts were intimately connected with his principles of commerce: trade not aid, loans not grants, aid for private enterprise to undercut the monopolistic powers of governments (whether Communist or non-Communist). However, this is not to argue that multilateralism can be considered *the* explanatory variable for Fulbright's cold war stance.

Belief 15: Conflict Can Be Mitigated by Education.

Peace by government was one strand of Fulbright's operational code, peace by consensus another. The sense of community necessary to secure peaceful adjustment of disputes could be awakened and maintained through international education.[12] There was an essential link between education, travel, the exchange of ideas, and the creation of world community. He himself had benefited from the Rhodes Scholarship program and from a grand tour of Europe. He had come to national attention as a young educator and saw international education as a civilizing influence on international politics. In 1945-1946, he assured a unique way of financing cultural exchange by transforming the "leftovers of war into instruments of peace" (Johnson and Colligan, 1965: 3). He firmly believed (U.S. Congress, 1946b: A4766) that the interchange of students between countries could play a major role in helping to break down mutual misunderstandings and in furthering the kind of knowledge that leads to mutual confidence. He came to believe that the exchange program was his greatest achievement; as late as 1969, he contended (Glad, 1969: 32), "The only creative thing I have done is the Educational Exchange Program." No longer believing that the best way to establish an international community was institutional, Fulbright advocated educational and psychological remedies. The danger of nuclear catastrophe made it mandatory, he believed, to utilize education to narrow the gap between human needs and the limited capacities of human nature (1966b).

The premise underlying his belief in education is that much of the conflict in the world is rooted in misunderstanding. Old myths are the culprits hindering understanding and must be discarded. From this premise it follows logically that education should not be at the periphery but at the center of international relations. Educational exchange could turn nations into people and could transform ideologies into human aspirations (1966a: 159-177). No matter how foolish and querulous a creature man may be, forever given to pernicious celebration of tribalism, Fulbright remains firm in his belief that the more accurately man recognizes his limitations the better his chance of transcending them.

OPTIMISM - PESSIMISM

Belief 16: Survival Is Contingent Upon Performance, Especially Upon U.S. Leadership in the Transformation of International Politics.

Belief 17: About the Ultimate Prospects of Mankind One Has To Be Optimistic, although Catastrophe Is an Ever-present Possibility.

Fulbright's optimism about the future resembles the conditional optimism of the biblical prophets. While he was a strong believer in the mission of the United States to civilize international politics, it was not enough to be chosen; redemption was conditional upon performance.

In the peace-by-government phase, the assurance of a peaceful world was predicated upon the American people making up their minds "to create a world in which war is no longer the accepted method of settling disputes" (U.S. Congress, 1943c: A477). If the American people would only realize its power and then wield it boldly and courageously instead of timidly and apologetically, the future was full of promise (U.S. Congress, 1944b: 572). His conditional optimism was also apparent in the belief in the intimate connection between world prosperity, peace, world trade, freedom, and stability. If the free enterprise vision triumphed, the future would be bright (U.S. Congress, 1945f: 7672).

As for the dangers of totalitarianism foreclosing the future, he made the outcome of the power struggle contingent on the external and internal behavior of the West. He believed (1949) that the cold war would continue for many years and that efforts to restrain the expansion of Communism were dependent on "continually combat[ting] the tendency to return to isolationism" as well as on education of the American people to accept "the necessity for positive guidance and assistance to other self-governing democracies." The Truman Doctrine, the Atlantic Pact, the Marshall Plan were cooperative measures with which the United States might "gradually be able to develop laws to which the Western nations at least will adhere, and which in time, if all the Western nations can stick together, will be accepted by the Russians" (Arkansas Gazette, 1949a).

The decisive shift in the world balance of power which he detected in 1963 and which would "permanently foreclose the possibility of significant Communist expansion" induced him to make a hopeful Wilsonian pronouncement on the long-run future (1963b: 27, 37). Fulbright's optimism was also apparent in his trust in the beneficence of Presidential supremacy in foreign affairs. In a speech on the Bricker Amendment (U.S. Congress, 1954: 1106), he put his trust in the Constitution as an instrument fit to deal with the perils ahead:

> I do not share the fears of an ignorant or willful President or Senate, and this faith on my part is not merely an innocent trust in individuals, present and future. It is a faith in the form of government which we have known for 165 years . . . and in the ability of our people, present and future, to regulate those institutions through the processes of government.

Fulbright's optimism in the future was frequently interspersed with pessimistic beliefs. He was far from believing that there was anything inevitable about U.S. success in foreign policy (1952):

> It may well be that history will prove that nothing can be done, but I am disposed to feel that there may be a way for us to assist other people to solve their problems. I expect that the experience we have had in the South during the past 30 years has influenced this belief on my part.

In 1945, Fulbright was troubled by the lack of firm commitment to internationalism he sensed in most of his colleagues and believed that they threw away "a second opportunity to help save the world and ourselves from self-destruction" (U.S. Congress, 1945h: 2896-2900). The near-unanimous vote for the United Nations Charter made him believe that the Senators did not understand the true implications of the document, that is, gradual sacrifices of U.S. sovereignty (U.S. Congress, 1945i: 7962).

The onset of the cold war convinced Fulbright that the United Nations could do little for peace and security in the short run. He was for bypassing the United Nations—the reason being that the United States had to act "because there is no one else to protect the rights of the United States" (1947a). In a gloomy invocation of the domino theory, he voiced his belief (U.S. Congress, 1947a: 3139) that if Greece and Turkey fell to the Communists, the door would be open to Asia and Africa. "If Africa, Asia, and Europe were subjected to the exclusive control we have come to know as the Iron Curtain, our future would indeed be dark." So pessimistic was Fulbright about the immediate outlook that in response to the Soviet-inspired elimination of Ferenc Nagy as Prime Minister of Hungary in May, 1947, he counseled against signing a peace treaty with Italy, since it involved the withdrawal of American troops. "The presence of our troops [in Italy] is a deterrent to the taking over of the Italian Government by the Russians" (U.S. Congress 1947b: 6248-6249).

The shock of Korea induced Fulbright (Arkansas Gazette, 1951a; Arkansas Democrat, 1951) to call for an early version of massive retaliation. Believing that the Korean War might be the opening round of a new aggressive phase of Soviet policy, he advocated use of the atomic bomb on Russia, provided the Soviet Union made an aggressive move in Western Europe or the Near East. Defining aggression, he subsumed under the term, "infiltration and fifth column activities designed to overthrow existing governments and establish new ones directed from Moscow." As to the area that should be protected by

American atomic might, he included Iran, Turkey, Greece, Yugoslavia, and the democratic nations of Western Europe, "If we don't use it [the atomic bomb], we are ruined. . . . I think it is foolish to assure Russia that we will not be the first to use the atomic bomb, I think we should let Russia think we might use it any minute."

In line with his pessimistic beliefs about the Soviet Union, he was unimpressed in 1955 with the "spirit of Geneva." Russia's switch from belligerence to friendliness was attributed by him to a failure of Communist efforts at worldwide subversion. In his judgment (Arkansas Gazette, 1955), the Russians had changed their tactics, not their long-term objectives. The Soviet economic and diplomatic offensive in the Middle East and Asia appeared to Fulbright to confirm his pessimistic estimates. When Dulles tried to discount the perils, Fulbright chided him for painting an unduly rosy picture of the Soviet Union. For the Senator, Russia was on the march, "talking treacherously in soft words . . . and losing no chance to preempt the cause of peace for its exploitation." Fulbright believed (U.S. Congress, 1956a: 3370) that from the standpoint of national security it was "safer to be pessimistic than to be overly optimistic."

Extreme pessimism is also apparent in Fulbright's response to De Gaulle's challenge of American leadership; in Fulbright's view, this was aimed at establishing a "third force" between the United States and the Soviet Union. A new European nationalism would represent the defeat of the West's highest hopes, and the "third force" concept was irresponsible nonsense. Invoking an almost Manichaean universe, Fulbright (1963b: 46-47) believed that the concept of "third force" rested

> on the faulty premise that the world struggle between communism and freedom is essentially a Soviet-American conflict. . . . There is in fact no such option open to any of the Atlantic nations unless one accepts the irrational proposition that it is possible to be neutral between one's friends and one's enemies.

More stoic beliefs about the prospects for realizing his conception of a world community came to the fore during the Vietnam crisis. Fulbright's working assumption was that one has to act as if, in the long run, redemption of history from the scourge of war, power politics, and the follies of man were possible. In this variation of an "as if" philosophy, optimism becomes a duty (Johnson and Gwertzman, 1968: 248).

In line with his professional duties in which too much gloom might be dysfunctional, he also believed (1966b) that

> our own human nature does not allow us to give up the game in advance, to reconcile ourselves to hopelessness or to death in a nuclear war. Our own human nature requires of us a certain faith in ourselves, an optimism which, unjustified though it may be, nonetheless must lead us to do what we can to feed the hungry, to cure the sick, to live in dignity and try to civilize the unrestrained competition of nations which threatens us with nuclear destruction.

PREDICTABILITY OF THE FUTURE

Belief 18: The Future Is in Part What We Make of It through Planning for It.

Belief 19: The Aim of Long-range Forecasting Is to Reduce Uncertainty by Establishing Alternatives with Some Chance of Getting Us to the Future We Want.

In accordance with a strong voluntaristic streak in his outlook, Fulbright believed in planning for the future, in anticipating events, in injecting a modicum of certainty into policy, in the efficacy of expertise. The belief in the predictability of the future was in part predicated upon his long-range optimism, in part dependent on the short-term fluctuations of American fortune.

Fulbright used various types of forecasting for various purposes.[13] In his peace-by-government phase (1943-1945), Fulbright's purpose in making predictions was "system replacement"; that is, the replacement of the nation-state system by a new system differing sharply from, and representing a substantial improvement over, the old one. The precise timing was left open, but the forecast claimed explicitly that some present and future events marked progress toward the replacement of the current system by the new one. What Fulbright envisaged was a system in which possession and use of power would be centralized, in which the law of a world community would proscribe those uses of power deemed incompatible with order, in which there would be clear criteria for differentiating law-breaking and law-enforcing uses of power. The Fulbright Resolution, the U.N. Charter, U.N.R.R.A., the Reciprocal Trade Act, the Bretton Woods Agreements, the Nuremberg Trials (U.S. Congress, 1945a: A3624), the atomic bomb—all become events pointing towards the new future. For example, the only solution he could conceive of (U.S. Congress, 1945e: A4654) with respect to the control of atomic weapons was

> the recognition, by all nations, that at last the time has arrived for all of us to delegate certain and definite powers over armaments to the United Nations Organization. Disputes of any kind relating to the subject should be under the compulsory jurisdiction of the international court, and every nation must be subject to the verdict of the court. If a nation, or individuals within a nation, should prove to be recalcitrant then the full power of the organization collectively and severally should be pledged to the enforcement of the judgment.
>
> To those who object that this is setting up a world government, I can only reply, call it what you will, there is no other principle with the slightest chance of success in the control of the atomic bomb.

While the onset of the cold war discredited what was fairly specific in Fulbright's forecasting, the vaguer aspects retained timeliness; he could repair to them by calling for a new kind of international relations, one in which the nation-state system would be overcome by functionalism, education, and psychological self-awareness.

Social mobilization is another type of forecast purpose. A dire future is invoked as almost inevitable unless immediate action is taken. The forecast also maintains that there is a great opportunity available to reach a promising future state of affairs. Fulbright engaged in a good many mobilization forecasts throughout his career. Indeed, he made his political reputation as a foreign policy expert in just that kind of activity when he joined others in the vast campaign to sell the United Nations to the American people.

His campaign for European unification is another example of his attempt at controlling the future by predicting it. Why was it so important to unite Europe? Fulbright predicted (1948a: 16) that "if Western Europe were to succumb to the Russians, that would imperil the Western Hemisphere."

Another purpose of forecasting is warning that a negative event will occur within the near future, unless remedial action is taken. Numerous examples are available. A few must suffice to make the point. During the Greek-Turkish crisis he warned (1947b):

> I have reached the conclusion that unless we are willing to do much more than we have up to date in the foreign field, communism will continue to spread and the power of Russia will become so great that, instead of cooperating, she will attempt to dictate to everyone. I believe that, if the United Nations is ever to grow into the kind of organization we hope that it will, no one

nation can be permitted to dominate the world so far as to become irresistible.

On the occasion of the Berlin Blockade, he predicted (Northwest Arkansas Times, 1948b), "If we stand up to the Russians, there's little likelihood of war. On the other hand, if we run away from them, we can hardly avoid one."

The above warnings were not unusual, given the climate of the times. One of the more striking predictions occurred in the Spring of 1954, when the U.S. government debated whether or not to intervene in Indochina. Few in Congress approved of intervention. One of the few was Senator Fulbright, who indicated, in an off-the-cuff remark to reporters (Arkansas Gazette, 1954), his support for sending ground troops to Indochina if it became necessary. "There isn't any other option unless we want to join up with the Communists."

CONTROL OF HISTORICAL DEVELOPMENT

Belief 20: Man Has Enough Power to Master, at Least in Part, His Destiny.

Belief 21: Great Capabilities Impose Great Responsibilities. The United States, As the Most Powerful Country, Has the Duty to Assume the Leadership in the Redemption of History (1943-1965).

Belief 22: The Power of Example is a Potent Redemptive Force in History (1966-).

What can be done about the unsatisfactory state of the international system? The answer depends partly on the estimates which national leaders make of their nation's adaptive capabilities in relation to the environment.[14] Fulbright believed in at least partial control of historical development but displayed varying estimates of the most appropriate means of control. Estimates ranged from control through centralized international institutions, to control through countervailing power, to control through a combination of U.S. example, regional pluralistic security communities, and gradualist enterprises, such as functionalism and education.

Fulbright displayed a high-capability estimate of the United States in his peace-by-government phase. Convinced of the efficacy of leadership at home and abroad, he believed in the United States' ability to bring about a transformation of the international system. Fulbright was sure of his country's obligation to exercise power in the redemption of history from the evils of power politics. He strongly believed (U.S. Congress, 1943d: 1012) that "this great nation of ours now has, or shortly will have, the power to turn this ghastly, barren tragedy into a tremendous opportunity, which, with imagination, intelligence, and determination, will enable us together with our allies to create the world of the future." He seemed to say that the United States can and therefore should affect the course of events around the globe. Why? "Not only are we rich and powerful but our success in self-government and our traditional abhorrence of aggression by violence has given us unique power of moral leadership among the nations of the world" (U.S. Congress, 1944b: 572).

Fulbright's original expectations that the anarchic nation-state system was convertible into a system with a single center of rule—perhaps a greatly strengthened United Nations as an alternative to the balance of power—were disappointed. He adapted himself to the necessity of coping with what he considered Soviet expansionism through means other than the United Nations. He concluded (Northwest Arkansas Times, 1946a) that the balance of power was the only solution to contain Russia. Indeed, if the United Nations had any chance at all to succeed eventually as a "voluntary union of peoples, it was imperative that . . . the existing power relationships among the great nations be preserved" (U.S. Congress, 1947c: 3137).

The assumption of controlling history with the balance of power was predicated upon a high estimate of U.S. power. Multilateral financial arrangements would secure enormous economic capabilities for the United States; high taxes and the military draft would secure strong armed forces (Arkansas Gazette, 1946). He believed especially in the beneficent mission of the Air Force to be "a stabilizing influence, particularly to prevent a rash move by the Russians" (Arkansas Gazette, 1953). Comparing the United States' role to Britain's in the 19th Century, he believed that "we must supply the force to keep the peace now as she did then, because we are the only country able and willing to do so" (Northwest Arkansas Times, 1949); and in 1951 (U.S. Congress, 1951b: 522), he summarized his belief in the efficacy of U.S. power as follows:

> I believe that our foreign policy should revolve around the basic assumption that the preservation of Western Europe from domination by Moscow is essential to our security and the long-term objective of establishing, eventually, a peaceful world of free men . . . . to refuse to accept the leadership and to provide the initia-

tive, when it is obvious that we alone among the free peoples have the power to provide both, seems to me to be tantamount to ultimate surrender.

The American mission of insuring peace in the world would be impaired by lack of Presidential leadership and by the uncertainty created whenever differences existed between the executive and the legislative branches of government. In Fulbright's view (Reporter, 1954a: 10), the performance of the Eisenhower administration and the isolationist segments of the Republican Party endangered "the role of leadership we are called upon to play among the free nations of the world. . . . there are many who are becoming more and more doubtful of our ability to govern ourselves . . . much less the democratic world and serve as a beacon light to guide the new and uncommitted nations."

Fulbright's belief about the way in which the American mission was to be achieved was thus circumscribed by his estimates of U.S. capabilities and leadership qualities. He was confident that if it were not for inept leadership, the United States could be master of its destiny.

Up to 1956, Fulbright regarded the balance of power as shifting in favor of the United States. Between 1956 and 1960, he appeared to discern a shifting of the global balance against the United States. The Kremlin appeared to demonstrate an unexpected technological prowess as well as success in the Third World. Clashes between Fulbright and Dulles must be understood in the context of an unfavorable shift in the balance of power and Fulbright's loss of confidence in Dulles' mastery of statecraft (U.S. Congress, 1956b: 3369, for example). Fulbright's differences with Dulles were thus partially rooted in different threat perceptions, with Fulbright believing that Dulles underestimated the Soviet threat (but see Stassen, 1972).

However, in the early 1960s, the balance again shifted in favor of the United States due to the completion of European recovery, the maintenance of American nuclear superiority, and the disappointment of Russian expectations of expansion in the Third World. Fulbright (1963b: 27) saw in the offing a "decisive shift in the world balance of power [which could] permanently foreclose the possibility of significant Soviet expansion." Secure in the impending success of the Atlantic community, he believed (1963b: 63) that

> our future depends less on what we do in confrontation with the Communist world than on the kinds of relations we develop and the kind of society we build within our own world. . . . our fu-

ture depends on whether we allow the West to succumb once again to divisive and destructive nationalism or whether we make it so strong and unified that no one will dare to attack us and so prosperous and progressive that it will serve as a model and a magnet for the entire world—for the struggling nations of Asia and Africa, for the unhappy peoples of Eastern Europe, and ultimately perhaps, for the Russians themselves.

This statement prompted Waltz (1965: 741) to remark bitingly that Fulbright's belief in conflict management through a preponderance of power amounted to aspiring to a "condition of world hegemony that would provide the material basis for managing the world without having achieved world government in form."

By 1966, Fulbright still held the premise (1966a: 256) that "America, as the most powerful nation, is the only nation equipped to lead the world in an effort to change the nature of politics," but the power he had in mind was no longer military and economic might. Redemption of history was to come through the power of example, since "rich and powerful though our country is, it is not rich or powerful enough to shape the course of world history in a constructive or desired direction solely by the impact of its power" (1968b: 156). The power of example was to be effective abroad by expanding the search for solutions to shared problems in such comparatively manageable areas as technological development, educational methods, and other functional enterprises. It also had domestic implications for the United States. In the biblical tradition, Fulbright, the prophet, exhorted his people to live up to the American mission of changing the nature of politics by giving up the "arrogance of power" and making their own society a shining example. "Inevitably and demonstrably, our major impact on the world is not what we do but what we are. It is the way we govern ourselves, the ideas about man and man's relations with other men that took root and flowered in the American soil" (1968b: 156-157). The uniqueness of the American purpose was still an article of faith for Fulbright (1967b: 30).[15]

THE ROLE OF CHANCE

Belief 23: War by Miscalculation Presents the Greatest Danger to Peace (1943-1964).

Belief 24: Miscalculation Can Be Reduced by Sharply Circumscribing the Right and Capacity of Nations for Self-help (1943-1945).

Belief 25: Miscalculation Can be Minimized by Making It Clear to Would-Be Aggressors that Aggression Would be Resisted by a Preponderance of Power (1943-1964).

Belief 26: War by Accident is Possible due to the Nature of Atomic Weapons (1958-).

Belief 27: War is Caused by Misperception (1964-).

Fulbright originally assumed that the risk of accidents in international affairs was negligible. Due to the strongly voluntaristic components of his operational code, aggression and war were associated not with unintentional human and mechanical errors but with conscious decisions of malfeasant policy makers who incorrectly forecast the amount of opposition they would face. Thus, war came about when the "lawless minority" in world affairs miscalculated. The most effective way to prevent war, then, is to create a condition in which the "lawless minority" in the world is never tempted to commit aggression (U.S. Congress, 1944a: A413). Miscalculation thus could be eliminated by sharply circumscribing the right and the capacity of nations for self-help through an international monopoly of force.

The cold war put an end to Fulbright's belief in the possibility of effective collective security machinery. Perceiving the Soviet Union as calculatingly bent upon aggression, the remedy was to make the limits of American tolerance unmistakably clear. In an early version of the Truman Doctrine, he warned (1946a: 51):

> There grew up after the last war the belief that our policy is peace at any price. I think Hitler believed this to be our policy and relied upon it. . . . Our present reluctance to maintain an army and a navy, together with the determined and articulate band of irreconcilable isolationists in our midst, may revive this belief. . . . it is highly important that all the world know that, while we do not seek war, yet we are willing and able to fight whenever we believe any power threatens the right and opportunity of men to live as free individuals under a government of their own choice

He believed that the North Atlantic Treaty was an effective means of avoiding Soviet miscalculations, since the development of the Pact would create such a preponderance of power in the West that "there would be practically no likelihood of any attack by Russia" (U.S. Congress, 1949: 3464, 9584). War could be prevented, then, by providing enough warning signals to would-be aggressors. These signals in the form of alliance commitments could not be tight enough for Fulbright (Arkansas Gazette, 1949b). The more automatic they were, the more effective he believed them to be. Not surprisingly, Fulbright endorsed collective security, Korean-style. While his first inclination was not to intervene, he "recalled what happened after Munich and the failure to take a strong position at that time. It is not only the immediate future which must be considered but we also must try to judge what the long-term developments will be" (1950b). Apparently, Fulbright was thinking in terms of nonsituational commitments which emphasized the general long-range interests inherent in the U.S. role as world leader. In this sense, U.S. commitments, especially to Europe, signified responsibility not just for the short-range, fluctuating security interests of the United States but the welfare of the West as a whole. The tighter the commitment, the greater the belief of others in the leadership qualities of the United States and the more unmistakable the warning to would-be aggressors.

Intimately connected with the belief in the efficacy of ironclad commitments was an image of the enemy which stressed its evil but not irrational character. Fulbright believed that "we will have to assume that those in the Kremlin are planning to advance over Europe." But since the Soviet moves "are the result of cold calculation, we will do well to follow their example" and establish clear warning signals in the form of commitments and indices of U.S. resolve to build an adequate defense for ourselves (U.S. Congress, 1951c: 64).

> I realize we are dealing with things which there is no way to prove ahead of time. But I believe that for the future of our own country, and for the moral standing of the United States . . . we must take the position that we will undertake to build a legitimate defense line in Western Europe. Otherwise, the effects would be disastrous to all free people.

The assumption of monolithicity of the Communist threat made it actually easier to believe in the efficacy of commitments. Fulbright (U.S. Congress, 1947c: 3137) viewed Communism as Soviet-directed, warning that the Soviet Union dominated Communist parties and their policies throughout the world; he believed the concentration of control in the Politburo in Moscow made Communism the real danger that it was.

In the late 1950s, however, Fulbright modified this belief and admitted the possibility that wars might begin unintentionally; he criticized (U.S. Congress, 1958b: 11845-11846) the doctrine of deterrence on the grounds that

> it depends on a degree of technical and human perfection which nothing in the experience of mankind leads us to expect. It is . . . irrational because of the very degree of rationality it requires . . . and the degree of control it presupposes [the U.S. and the U.S.S.R.] exercise over developments throughout the world.

Thus, accidental and catalytic wars appeared possible.

Beginning in 1964, the role of misunderstanding as a cause of war and tension began to dominate Fulbright's operational code. He argued (1964a: 28) against the "master myth" of the cold war, namely that "the Communist bloc is a monolith composed of governments which are not really governments at all, but organized conspiracies, divided among themselves perhaps on certain matters of tactics, but all equally resolute and implacable in their determination to destroy the free world." He believed (1964a: 28) in variations, "ranging from China, which poses immediate threats to the free world, to Poland and Yugoslavia, which pose none." He also believed that using oversimplified historical analogies distorted American thinking about foreign policy. Preoccupied with the memories of appeasement in the interwar period, some of the highest officials in the government seemed to have no doubt that a compromise peace in Southeast Asia would amount to another Munich (1967c).

Since Fulbright's major concern was no longer possible miscalculation by the Soviet Union or other Communist countries but by his own government, he began to believe that U.S. policymakers would do well to heed the advice of psychologists against the dangers of black-and-white thinking, the creation of diabolical enemy-images, the self-fulfilling prophecy. Miscalculation, then, would be controlled by empathy, understanding, and mutual role-taking.

FULBRIGHT'S OPERATIONAL CODE: INSTRUMENTAL BELIEFS

SELECTING GOALS FOR POLITICAL ACTION

Belief 28: An International Community-Oriented Approach to Foreign Affairs Implies Deflating the Cult of Sovereignty.

Belief 29: A Senator's First Responsiblility in Foreign Affairs Is to Protect the Executive from Irrational Domestic Forces.

Belief 30: A Power Approach to International Politics Implies that Finite Resources Must be Brought to Bear in Strategic Areas.

Belief 31: A Low-posture Approach to Foreign Affairs Implies Deflating the Cult of Presidential Omniscience.

Fulbright's advocacy of the proper U.S. foreign policy role was heavily influenced by his image of the predominant enemy of rationality in international politics and the concomitant image of the structure of the international system. In his international community-oriented approach, he believed that the proper national role for the United States was to be the reformist leader in the transcendence of power politics. The United States was assigned the role of redeemer from the scourge of an anarchical international system. Effective international organization would become the promoter, the expression, and the instrument of an ultimately global community.

Fulbright's belief in the proper amount of Presidential authority became primarily a function of three variables: his image of the enemy, his capability judgments, and his confidence in the wisdom of the Executive in foreign affairs. It stood to reason for Fulbright that if the enemy were aggressive totalitarianism and if the international system were unstable and yet tightly interdependent, the President must be freed from legislative obstructionism so as to be able to respond promptly to change. This meant that American backsliding into isolationism had to be avoided. Initially, protection of the Executive from the forces of irrationalism was to be achieved through constitutional reform in the British image—Presidential and Congressional power of dissolution, more disciplined parties (both in power and in opposition), and a question-and-answer period in the Senate (U.S. Congress, 1947d: 334; 1948: 9996-9997; 1945k: 81). Fulbright's efficiency-oriented beliefs were also directed toward curbing the Senate's treaty power. He introduced a resolution in the Senate suggesting that the Constitution be amended to require ratification of treaties by a simple majority vote in both houses of Congress (U.S. Congress, 1945l: 232; Northwest Arkansas Times, 1945). Subsequent heavy majorities for the U.N. Charter put an end to this type of constitutional amendment.

In his vigorous support for the U.S. policy of containment and therefore of the treaty system constructed between 1946 and 1955, Fulbright generally supported the most generous interpretation possible of Presidential authority and opposed all attempts to cast doubts on the firmness of U.S. commitments and Presidential ability to react swiftly to any threat. He came out squarely against the diminution of what he considered Presidential prerogative (U.S. Congress, 1951c: 520).

> The issue is whether the President should seek the advice of Congress . . . or whether his discretion should be subject to the consent of Congress. He [the President] is not willing . . . to accept the principle that the consent of Congress is necessary to validate his decision.
> Personally, I agree with the position of the President.

In the long run, decisions of military strategy were best left to the Executive. That, he believed, was the plain intent of the Constitution. He also believed (U.S. Congress, 1951d: 520) that "it would be dangerous for our future welfare to change the underlying principle simply because a strong minority or even a majority of the Congress may lack confidence in the wisdom of the Executive in some particular instance."

The fight against isolationism reached its height in the debate on the Bricker Amendment in 1954. Fulbright sternly counseled those who were inspired by their suspicion of executive power that the Constitution should not be misused to paralyze that power when international responsibilities imperatively demanded the strengthening, not the weakening, of the executive branch (U.S. Congress, 1954: 1106).

> Our enemy is not the President of the United States, whether the incumbent, his successor to come, or his predecessors . . . . It was never intended by the Founding Fathers that the President of the United States should be a ventriloquist dummy sitting on the lap of the Congress.

Senator Fulbright's endeavor to increase the foreign affairs powers of the President cannot be properly understood without reference to Senator Joseph McCarthy. Fulbright was trying to shield the Executive from the disruptive influence of what he called the "swinish blight of anti-intellectualism" so malignantly personified by McCarthy. Fulbright's emphasis on Presidential primacy in foreign policy was intended to serve as a counterweight to the unilateral forces in the country and in Congress, whether McCarthyism, the Bricker Amendment movement, or any other manifestations of distrust of authority, institutions, and expert knowledge in foreign affairs.

How can the demands of efficiency in the formulation and execution of American foreign policy be reconciled with an independent legislature? With the accession to the Chairmanship of the Senate Foreign Relations Committee in 1959, Fulbright had reached a position of influence from which to make felt his beliefs as to the appropriate mix of efficiency and accountability of the Executive. Hope was high that under the vigorous leadership of a young Chairman, the Foreign Relations Committee would become a pillar of Congressional involvement in foreign affairs, as it had been during the years 1945-1955. The hopes were disappointed. Overwhelmed by the complexity of the subject matter, Fulbright believed that the proper strategy to deal with foreign affairs was to place the Senate outside the mainstream of the foreign policy process (U.S. Congress, 1959b: 6193). As he put it (Reporter, 1959: 24):

> The Senate, by keeping its distance from the Executive, can be an effective instrument of public education; it can define and clarify the zones of the feasible, the areas of the negotiable, thereby assuring that the Executive, when it decides to act, has the fullest support of public opinion. On its own, moreover, the Senate can bring its social inventiveness into play by formulating the policy objectives to be pursued around the world, while leaving the Executive complete freedom as to the timing and tactics. In other words, the function of the Senate, and of the Foreign Relations Committee in particular, is to try to be the conscience of the Executive—without in any way indulging in the frivolous delusion of co-equality.

In practice, Fulbright's theory meant that he was not informed of Khrushchev's visit to the United States before the public announcement, nor was he informed in advance of President Eisenhower's intention to go to Europe. However, Fulbright did not consider this an affront to the dignity of the Senate Foreign Relations Committee.

Fulbright conceded a minor initiative role to Congress, which he believed (1959) "can often come up with ideas on the periphery of foreign affairs which the big policy makers would never have the imagination nor the mother wit to conceive." Thus, Fulbright regarded the constitutional and practical role of the Senate as essentially negative, that of a legitimator of major policies and occasional initiator of marginal ones.

Fulbright sharply differentiated between the making of foreign policy based upon expertise in the executive branch and the public discussion of long-range, basic problems of foreign policy by the Senate (Vital Speeches, 1959: 527-532). The Foreign Relations Committee would become the constituency for the future and would not interfere with the short-range diplomatic business of the Executive. He was concerned then with establishing a relationship between what the United States was doing and where it was going, in the hope that better understanding of this relationship would make for greater predictability of the future. This was in tune with the model of rational foreign policy making, since it had the effect of shielding the Executive from unpleasant inquiries into details (where, as is well known, the devil hides).[16]

Apparently, the model in Fulbright's mind for the role of the Foreign Relations Committee was the Joint Economic Committee. The latter's primary function was to study and give advice on broad areas of policy, but it had no substantive powers. Had the Foreign Relations Committee become a foreign policy version of the Joint Economic Committee, it would indeed have dealt with the long-range basic questions of defining major problems, priorities, and alternative solutions, but it would have abdicated its oversight function, that is to say, it would have abdicated from politics.[17]

How could the Foreign Relations Committee be an educational institution? First, as Chairman, Fulbright would make a systematic endeavor "to promote a better two-way communications channel between government and the universities especially at the policy level—in an attempt to spur the rate at which ideas can flow directly from the universities to the practicing politicians," and secondly, the Committee would promote a series of informal exchanges between outstanding scholars in the field of foreign affairs and members of the Senate (Vital Speeches, 1959a: 531).

As for the usefulness of the research farmed out by the Committee, the response was mixed (Halperin, 1960; Robinson, 1960). The thick volumes did not enhance the oversight capabilities of the Senate, but they fit in with Fulbright's conception of the Committee's proper role as interpreter of long-range trends.

De-emphasis of the oversight function was also evident in Fulbright's various attempts to bypass the Appropriations Committees and authorize the Executive to borrow foreign aid funds on a long-term basis directly from the Treasury. Fulbright could see no great virtue in the fact that the two-step procedure of authorizations plus appropriations gives greater control to Congressional committees (Senate Committee on Foreign Relations, 1959: 20).

In sum, as long as the United States was confronted with adversaries able to focus unrestrained personal power and vast resources on the advancement of a grand design, Fulbright (1961a: 12; 1963b: 106, 116) called for "conferral of greatly increased authority on the President . . . for he alone can act to mobilize our power and resources toward the realization of clearly defined objectives and to wean the American people and their representatives from the luxuries of parochialism and self-indulgence." The conclusion is inescapable that Fulbright believed Congress had too much power in foreign affairs, while the President did not have enough. Given this belief, it was not surprising that he was inimical to Congressional attempts to counterattack in the perennial struggle to influence foreign policy in the fields of more effective administrative oversight and authorizations. Predicated as this role conception was upon the permeability of the decision-making process, "closed politics" would bring about its bankruptcy, as developments in Vietnam demonstrated.

Fulbright believed that, as leader of the free world, the United States had the capability to control the security destiny of the West by balancing the international system through bypassing the United Nations, maintaining bloc cohesion, defending the peace through collective defense arrangements, and guiding change along constructive lines by developing the Third World. In this anti-Communist version of Wilsonianism, peace was still theoretically indivisible. The United States was the executor of collective security—with collective legitimization, if possible; without it, if necessary.

However, a power approach to international politics, even when Fulbright was at his most sanguine about American capabilities, did not mean that all corners of the globe were of equal strategic importance. In matters of global priorities, Fulbright generally was a Europe-firster and called for U.S. participation in Western European defense in addition to the defense of the Western hemisphere. With respect to other critical strategic areas, such as Turkey, Greece, and Japan, he advocated assistance to their efforts to resist Russian aggression within the limits of available American resources. Since he did not invariably believe that every small territorial grab in secondary and tertiary areas would add up to a major shift in the balance of power and invite a domino effect, he called for flexibility in the correction of local imbalances (Arkansas Gazette, 1951b). An example necessitating flexibility was Korea, where he advocated withdrawal after the Chinese intervention (U.S. Congress, 1951e: 521):

> We should not undertake at this time a major land war with China. If this is the beginning of World War III, we must not

forget that the Kremlin is the primary enemy and China merely a satellite. . . . In spite of the valid principle which we sought to support, we should not jeopardize the military security of the free world by pursuing an impracticable undertaking.

Similar discrimination was apparent in Fulbright's beliefs about the dangers posed by the Castro regime. In a famous memorandum to President Kennedy, he advised against invasion of Cuba in 1961 and advocated toleration. However, the memorandum contained an important proviso. The United States could afford to tolerate Castro "provided that the Soviet Union uses Cuba only as a political and not as a military base ('military' is used here to mean missiles and nuclear weapons, not small conventional arms)" (Meyer, 1963: 195-205). As long as the Soviet Union did not use Cuba to effect a significant change in the global balance of power," the Castro regime is a thorn in the flesh; but it is not a dagger in the heart." The thorn was transformed into a dagger in the fall of 1962, with the advent of the Cuban missile crisis. Fulbright was all for removing the missiles. Indeed, together with Senator Richard Russell (D., Georgia), he advocated the invasion of Cuba by American forces (1966a:48).

In 1966, the role Fulbright believed appropriate for the United States was still one of leadership in the effort to civilize international politics through various functional enterprises. However, it was a "low posture" leadership through example rather than intervention. Fulbright believed the United States no longer had the adaptive capabilities to achieve its purpose in the manner used during the period of U.S.-controlled internationalism. In an international system moving toward multipolarity, with nationalism considered a stronger force than Communism, local Communist triumphs would no longer necessarily change the world balance of power.

Fulbright's stance in 1966 again exhibited a high degree of international community-orientedness, as indicated by his rediscovery of the U.N., his belief that the United States must channel its internationalism through international organizations, his renewed emphasis on the obsolescence of the nation-state, and his emphasis on functionalism and education as a way to civilize the nation-state system. What differentiated his stance in 1966 and afterwards from his 1945 stance of community-orientedness was primarily his pessimistic estimate of U.S. capabilities to bring about a reform of the international system through active intervention. Both were postures of leadership on the part of the United States, one through structural transformation, the other through example. Both were equally authentic beliefs in the

U.S. obligation to regenerate mankind. The corollary of low-posture leadership in foreign affairs was a re-accentuation of priorities from hyperactivity abroad to the primacy of domestic politics. In practical terms, he also believed now that the policy sector favored in resource allocation should no longer be foreign but domestic.

Changes in beliefs about the nature of the enemy and about U.S. capabilities had important implications for Fulbright's beliefs about proper Congressional-Presidential relationships in foreign affairs. The belief change came about gradually in response to events in 1964 (Gulf of Tonkin incident) and 1965 (Dominican intervention). In 1964, Fulbright still denied (U.S. Congress, 1964c: 18458, 18462) that the Senate had more than an advisory role to play: "Our role is one of an advisory nature. Information is submitted to the committee. The administration has never held anything back, to my knowledge. . . . We have an opportunity to advise them, and that is all. We cannot direct or force them." More doubt is apparent in Fulbright's response to the contemplated introduction of American ground troops into South Vietnam in March, 1965. "The President," he commented (1965b: 9), "is in this difficulty, and we have to support him, I suppose." He also believed that, because of the critical conditions in Vietnam, a public debate of Vietnam in the Senate Foreign Relations Committee would serve no good purpose. Fulbright's September 15, 1965, speech on the Dominican intervention was still not conceived by him as posing an institutional challenge to the President; he was simply reasserting that he believed in free speech for Senators, including the Chairman of the Senate Foreign Relations Committee (U.S. Congress, 1965b: 28390-391). The collapse of the administration's credibility, brought about by its heavy-handed methods in attempting to win public support for the Dominican intervention, had important implications for Fulbright. A government that had displayed such an appalling lack of expertise in the Carribbean might have perhaps even less accurate information as to what precisely was happening in such a far-away theater as Vietnam.

With Fulbright's confidence in expertise shattered, he became receptive to the idea of challenging the administration's policy objectives publicly in a series of hearings in 1966. Interestingly enough, the distinction Fulbright made between long-range basic goals and specialized knowledge for implementation of goals enabled him to assert that the judgment of trained elites was no more valid than the judgment of an educated people. There were no experts in the choice of basic goals. Since he believed that the crisis over Vietnam was caused by confusion over basic objectives sought there, he assumed that it was his duty to educate the people to become competent judges of the administration. Equipped with countervailing information, the American people would acquire the capacity to pass judgment on "whether the massive deployment and destruction of their men and their wealth seems to serve their over-all interest as a nation" (1966c: xii). Thus, belief in the educability of the public (and of Fulbright) was predicated upon the belief that officials of the executive branch had no special insights based on special information (1966c: 70).

Fulbright's belief that the true dissenter dissents about purpose and not method, was in consonance with his dualistic differentiation between long-term judgments and short-term expertise, and his deflation of the "cult of executive expertise." It did not yet revive the oversight function of the Foreign Relations Committee, based as this function necessarily is on specific counter-expertise in the details of policy. His comment (U.S. Congress, 1966a: 1943) was revealing:

> There is no possible way for the Senate—we can't have a department of our own, a C.I.A. of our own. . . . We have 6 overworked professional staff members on my committee and we have always traditionally relied upon the administration and I think we always will. . . . our function isn't to duplicate the State Department and the C.I.A.

However, the change in Fulbright's belief about executive competence had already taken effect in 1966-67 on specific issues. Most conspicuous was his lead in restricting foreign aid authorizations to one year (U.S. Congress, 1966b: 16021, 17066; 1966c: 232-237), and his refusal of President Johnson's request for advance commitments for Latin American aid (U.S. Congress, 1967: 7058-7059). By 1967, Fulbright had even joined the few Senators determined to attack the most sacred cow of national security policy, the defense budget (Congressional Quarterly 1967: 312-313).

Fulbright's undue pessimism about the possibility of developing counter-expertise is shown by subsequent developments. By the end of the 1960s, Fulbright's operational-code change with regard to the proper relationship between President and Senate had spread to the oversight area, where for the first time in decades Congress sought to exercise a "truly independent critical judgment of proposals on foreign and defense policy questions" (New York Times, 1971).

PURSUIT OF GOALS

Belief 32: Drift Is the Greatest Sin in Foreign Policy.

Belief 33: Do Not Pursue Indefinitely Goals that Are Completely Hopeless, but Rather than Giving Up a Goal Completely, Try to Realize It at a Smaller Scale and/or with Different Means.

Belief 34: Private Influence Must Precede Public Dissent, Especially When the President Exerts Strong Leadership.

Belief 35: Delegation of Senatorial Foreign Affairs Authority to the Executive Branch Is Contingent upon Performance.

Belief 36: Presidential-Congressional Relations Must be Based on Institutional rather than Personal Judgment.

In tune with his activist philosophy of foreign affairs, Fulbright associated isolationism with Congress and collective security with the Presidency (U.S. Congress, 1945m: A3623). To go on the attack in foreign policy was the proper strategy, since, as he believed (1942), "we must make this war creative just as we made the depression creative and not simply defensive. No game is really won by remaining on the defensive." Yet he came to suspect that the government did not really know what it was doing and was just drifting along with events. "We improvise from day to day and the people who do the improvising have very little qualification" (1945c). Muddling through, he believed (1945d), was the greatest shortcoming of U.S. foreign policy. The government had lost its bearings and was "drifting in a fog of indecisiveness" (U.S. Congress, 1945d: 10963).

As for pursuing goals that had become hopeless of attainment, Fulbright did not believe in chasing after chimera. As a member of the Senate, he felt (1953b) he was justified in confining his attention to those matters "which are at least within the realm of the possible and attainable within the foreseeable future." Whether it was the building up of the security functions of the United Nations or the unification of Europe, he was aware of the risks of the great design when conditions were not ripe. For example, in analyzing the Article 19 crisis in 1964-1965, he pointed out the risks in strengthening international law when political conditions are militating against it. "It is simply not realistic, under existing world conditions, to expect any great power, including the United States, to support and finance an international peacekeeping expedition to which it fundamentally objects" (1965c). He believed that "attempts to outrun history were unrewarding"; eventually, he perceived (1965c) that the limited opportunities to reform and adapt the multistate system to the requirements of the nuclear age were not found "in general programs for world law under powerful international institutions," but in the field of practical cooperation between nations on specific projects. Thus, Senator Fulbright's journey, which began with the bang of structural reform of the international system between 1943 and 1945, seemed to end with the whimper of functionalism. This meant that rather than giving up the goal of world community completely, he tried to realize it at a smaller scale (European federal unity up to the early 1950s) and/or with different means (functional rather than structural enterprises).

It is evident that in general Fulbright believed in utilizing institutionalized channels, depending on whether or not he expected success in influencing the Executive privately (Johnson and Gwertzman, 1968: 180-181). This be believed was more likely when a strong Democratic President occupied the White House. He hesitated for quite some time to voice his doubts about Vietnam publicly, because he believed that he would be able to convince President Johnson privately to stay away from escalation (Johnson and Gwertzman, 1968: 205-206). Ultimately, of course, he failed to persuade the President to follow a different course in Vietnam. When he realized this, he reluctantly left the "President's team" and carried his case to the public, hoping that the attitudes of the people and especially their votes would change the President's mind.

When Fulbright believed that leadership in the White House was weak and the policies pursued disastrous, he did not hesitate to go immediately to the public to make his case. The most instructive example for this is his opposition to President Eisenhower's 1957 request for special grants of authority in a joint resolution showing American firmness in the Middle East. The handling of the Aswan Dam financing by Secretary Dulles, the apparent success of the Soviet economic offensive, the Suez crisis, and Hungary had convinced Fulbright that the policies of the administration were deficient. Congress engaged in a two-month debate of the Eisenhower Doctrine, and Fulbright led the attack upon the Republican administration. The debate was carried on in constitutional terms although it was clear that Fulbright's constitutional conscience was aroused by his extreme dissatisfaction with Dulles. The catalogue of particulars included grievous wounding of

America's old allies, France and Great Britain, making policies disastrous to the West and NATO, unwarranted promises by the Secretary. Fulbright believed that in order to justify voting for the resolution, "one must indeed have a full and deep confidence in those who are to administer such far-reaching powers"; he needed "more convincing evidence . . . that the Secretary of State had evolved policies regarding the Middle East which are in the interest of our national security" (Senate Committee on Foreign Relations and Committee on Armed Services, 1957a: 28, 217-218).

Fulbright's opposition to the Eisenhower Doctrine was a constitutionally draped vote of no confidence in the foreign policy of the Republican administration. But Fulbright's case was weak because he did not differ with the administration on the gravity of the threat and was even prepared (U.S. Congress, 1957: 2317) to vote for a simple or concurrent sense resolution, which would go beyond the administration's wording of opposing "overt armed aggression" and include "aggression by any other means."

In the end, it was this very rule of basing Presidential-Congressional relations on personal rather than institutional judgment that made him an easy target for President Johnson during the Gulf of Tonkin crisis. No one described the fundamental weakness of this rule more eloquently than Fulbright himself (Senate Committee on the Judiciary Subcommittee on Separation of Powers, 1967: 47):

> The error of those of us who piloted this resolution through the Senate . . . was in making a personal judgment when we should have made an institutional judgment. . . . we did not deal with the resolution in terms of what it said and in terms of the power it would vest in the Presidency; we dealt with it in terms of how we thought it would be used by the man who occupied the Presidency. Our judgment turned out to be wrong, but even if it had been right . . . the abridgement of the legislative process and our consent to so sweeping a grant of power was not only a mistake but a failure of responsibility on the part of the Congress.

CALCULATION AND CONTROL OF RISKS

Belief 37: Risks of Action Can be Minimized by Not Becoming a Captive of Blueprints.

Belief 38: Inextricable Commitment on the Asian Continent Must be Avoided.

Belief 39: The Risks of Executive Dominance in Foreign Affairs Can be Checked by a Strong Legislature.

In advocating a buildup of United Nations security functions, Fulbright chided the blueprinters for paying too much attention to detail. In one of his then-characteristic statements of hope that the future would spell out its own details, he voiced the belief (1943: 218) that "in venturing into the uncharted realm of international controls, it would be a mistake to attempt a complete blueprint which would later prove too restrictive." A similar reluctance to circumscribe the future is evident in Fulbright's various resolutions on a United Europe, in which he never attempted to define the scope of a European federation. His belief that amendments of the U.N. Charter were a waste of time also testifies to his misgivings about formal detail. As he opined in a letter to Ben V. Cohen (1954b):

> I have been a little bothered about the movement on the part of many of my friends to amend the Charter. It seems to me that Americans have a great weakness for passing laws and amending charters rather than striving to understand and improve the measures we already have.

Similarly, he interpreted the principle of sovereignty in the Charter as being unfortunate if it meant the preservation of the status quo, but acceptable if it meant an agreement not to use the power of the organization "to destroy the identity, the culture, and the independence of the various members by force" (U.S. Congress, 1945b: 2899). Essentially, then, the risks of action would be minimized by transforming in a step-by-step procedure a system of unlimited sovereignty into a federal order characterized by the fact that crucial decisions must be arrived at cooperatively between autonomous parties to the federal compact.

Previously, we indicated that Fulbright believed advance commitments, protected by a stance of inflexibility, would be effective in frustrating aggression. However, the risk of inflexibility of commitments was tempered by differentiating between major and minor enemies and by a reluctance to see the United States become engaged in a major land war in Asia. He did not want to see the country getting bogged down in a "land war with the masses of Asia when our real enemy is Russia" (1951b). In this context, he believed it the better part of wisdom to make decisions "in accordance with calculations as to what the potential enemy is capable of doing, rather than attempting to guess what he will do" (1951c). Faced with major opposition in a tertiary or even secondary theater, the United States had better retreat to preserve its power for the major showdown with the major enemy.

The belief that small operations to combat aggression in peripheral areas are appropriate but that large-scale engagements are a dissipation of forces was also valid for Fulbright in South Vietnam. In 1961, he came out in support of the administration position in Vietnam. First, he spoke out against those who wanted the United States to commit its strength anywhere outside the Communist empire. This was dangerous because "nothing would please Communist leaders more than to draw the United States into costly commitments of its resources to peripheral struggles in which the principal Communist powers are not themselves directly involved." He singled out Laos as an example of the incorrect kind of commitment (U.S. Congress, 1961c: 11702-11703). Hence, the proper course of U.S. action was to sustain efforts of the Vietnamese army to cope effectively with the hit-and-run activities of the guerrillas while devoting at least as much effort to assisting and guiding the Vietnamese people in their struggle for dignity and economic independence. In 1964, Fulbright still insisted that "we have no choice but to support the South Vietnamese Government" and warned cryptically (1964a: 43-44) that "it should be clear to all concerned that the United States will continue to defend its vital interests with respect to Vietnam." His eventual dissent to Johnson's escalation in Vietnam can be partially explained by the President's violation of Fulbright's rule of only limited opposition to Communist advances in peripheral areas.

In the "arrogance of power" phase, the actions of the Chief Executive rather than those of the Communists were the objects of control. The risks inherent in the loss of contact with reality Fulbright detected in the White House, reinforced by organizational discipline and the cult of expertise, and amounting to a de facto dictatorship of the President over the conduct of foreign affairs, could be controlled by the hurdles of Congressional processes. Rational policy was out, bureaucratic politics were in:

> A legislature serves a society as much by what it delays or prevents as by what it expedites or enacts . . . the apparent belief that decision is always better than delay and action better than inaction [is] a dubious assumption indeed, rooted in a Panglossian view of human nature (1972: 240).

TIMING

Belief 40: Great Opportunities for Reform Exist after Great Upheavals.

Belief 41: Negotiate from Strength Only.

Immediately during or after great upheavals is the time for the presentation and adoption of important new measures. This was true for the United States in 1944, when bipartisan agreement made it advisable to push for major legislation to insure U.S. participation in an international organization; and it was true with respect to inducing the European countries to unite before they had recovered from the war.

Fulbright also had an acute sense of timing when it came to negotiations. For example, he was against premature disarmament of the United States (1945e). "We should not eliminate ourselves as a great military power before the international organization, whatever it may be, is definitely established and some understanding arrived at with the other major nations." He was also against turning over control of the atomic bomb to the United Nations before it was strengthened enough to fulfill its functions properly. "I have a distinct feeling that it would be a psychological mistake for us to lead off by a definite decision not to maintain a powerful army," because "there is some bargaining power with the other nations in keeping our policy indefinite at this particular point" (1945f).

In Europe, the time to act was now (1948a: 12, 35; Senate Committee on Foreign Relations, 1949a: 84); in other areas, Fulbright displayed a fine sense for slowing down. In the area of colonialism, for example, he doubted it would be feasible to use pressure on the colonial powers to make them comply with U.S. wishes (1945g). It was one thing to use ECA funds to pressure European countries into unification; it was quite another matter to use ECA funds to pressure the Dutch into compliance with a U.N. resolution on their colonies.

Concerning the prerequisites for successful negotiations, Fulbright generally fit into the peace-through-strength category. Successful negotiations were conditional, in his judgment, upon the ability of the West to frustrate the aggressive and universalistic designs of Soviet leaders.

Interesting examples of his sense of timing are provided by the Vietnam War. In 1964 (1964a: 42), Fulbright believed negotiations out of the question since the United States' bargaining position was weak in view of the military circumstances: "until equation of advantages between the 2 sides has been substantially altered in our favor, there can be little prospect of a negotiated settlement which would secure the independence of a non-Communist South Vietnam." He also found it premature to engage the United Nations in South Vietnam since "things have been going so badly against the forces of the independent South Vietnamese Government that I doubt that it would be feasible to seek to bring the United Nations into that operation at the present time" (U.S. Congress, 1964d: 14792).

ROLE AND UTILITY OF DIFFERENT MEANS

Belief 42: Nonmilitary Foreign Policy Tools are More Effective than Military Ones.

Belief 43: Multilateral Agencies are More Effective than Bilateral Ones.

Belief 44: The Purpose of Dissent is to Create a New Universe of Discourse.

Rather than assessing the whole gamut of means Fulbright uses in his foreign policy work, we shall concentrate on two tools which are fairly representative—foreign aid and rhetoric.

In Fulbright's search for relevant nonmilitary foreign policy tools to shape an international environment where changes would occur in a peaceful, orderly manner, he initially accepted the basic assumptions of U.S. development policy—trade liberalization, promotion of private investment, reliance on indigenous domestic efforts, and limited orthodox lending through American-controlled international financial institutions which would base their loan policies on sound business practices. Thus, loans rather than grants were appropriate economic tools. He believed, for example, that the Marshall Plan should utilize loans for specific purposes (1947e), although he acquiesced eventually in the grant approach for the European program. Thus, in the loan-grant controversy so prominent in the debates on foreign aid, Fulbright shared the general hostility of Congress toward grants, with the exception of technical assistance where relatively small sums were involved. He believed in the efficacy of the Point 4 program, primarily because of its educational aspects and liked to compare it with the

Agricultural Extension Service (U.S. Congress, 1951f: 10852):

> In the long run . . . [Point 4] contains more promise than anything else we are doing, especially when we consider it along with the program of the exchange of persons. . . . joined together . . . they can do a great deal to weld the free peoples together into an effective union.

Technical assistance was very close to the heart of agriculturalists from the rural states, "because we are so familiar with the work of the county agent. All the county agents did was to bring the farmer knowledge of modern methods." During the Truman era, then, the Senator was by and large in agreement with administration policy, although he differed with it in a number of nuances. He believed (with the administration) that trade liberalization and aid were alternative instruments of foreign economic policy and that less aid would be necessary if American trade barriers were lowered. He supported the administration's judgment that Europe be given priority in assistance over Asia. As for aid to Europe, he believed that aid ought to be used to bring about unification rather than mere economic reconstruction. He also did not hesitate to use the Marshall Plan to further Arkansas economic interests. Arkansas aluminum, cane syrup, mules, wooden handles were all worthy products to be unloaded on Europe, since "the least they [ECA administrators] can do is use some reason in this program and distribute part of the purchases to our domestic companies."

He believed also that increased emphasis on military rather than economic aid was detrimental to American interests. His dissatisfaction with overemphasis on military aid became especially pronounced when he began to perceive the cold war as a long-term economic competition in the Third World. He strongly believed that economic growth would enable governments of underdeveloped countries to resist both internal demands for adoption of a Communist-type system and external demands by the Soviet Union or Communist China. Fulbright became one of the major critics of what he considered the overmilitarized response of the Eisenhower administration to the cold war. At the same time, he became a staunch ally in administration attempts to establish the Development Loan Fund, which was to become the primary agency for soft lending and long-term financing.

In the great 1956 foreign aid debate, the Millikan-Rostow thesis emerged as the leading intellectual argument and was strongly endorsed by Fulbright. The thesis basically stated that national interest required a long-range economic development program based on strictly economic criteria and divorced as much as possible from political and military considerations, although conceived to serve the long-run interests of American security. Particularly appealing to Fulbright was the sharp differentiation of the new rationale between short-term and long-run political objectives of foreign aid and the separation of military aid from economic aid. In matters military, judgments had to be made regarding the probability of armed conflict, and military aid was dependent on those guesses which only the President could make. But it was different with economic development. "Here is a job to be done. The determining factor is not some vague . . . judgment . . . but here is country X. It can reasonably absorb and make progress under a certain program which qualified people can estimate" (Senate Special Committee to Study the Foreign Aid Program, 1957b: 80-81).

Fulbright believed that the most distasteful feature of the old aid approach was its short-run power political implications, which would disturb progress of the recipient society in a satisfactory rate of growth toward a self-sustaining basis. Other interesting beliefs were that those who had experience in the development of Arkansas were uniquely qualified as observers of underdeveloped areas, because Arkansas had been "a colonial appendage of the northeastern part of the United States since the civil war;" a sharp differentiation between the Soviet foreign aid objective—"theirs is to make these countries dependent upon themselves and in many cases to disrupt their economy"—and the American objective—"ours is to be constructive and to make these countries independent;" and a strong conviction that without U.S. assistance, the Third World would go Communist and the balance of power would shift disastrously against the United States (Senate Special Committee to Study the Foreign Aid Program, 1957b: 240, 241, 380).

As for dispensing foreign aid funds through multilateral institutions Fulbright supported the World Bank and its offshoots, the International Finance Corporation and the International Development Association, as well as the Inter-American Development Bank—agencies which did not include Communist nations as members and in which, through a combination of weighted voting and the predominance of American personnel, strong American influence was insured. As late as 1961, Fulbright considered the International Bank for Reconstruction and Development an "independent agency, not a specialized agency of the United Nations." Not unexpectedly, he opposed SUNFED and in general all schemes which would have decreased the influence of the World Bank in international public finance, but he was dangerous because "nothing would please Communists leaders Committee on Foreign Relations, 1961: 413).

During the Kennedy administration, under the impact of the deteriorating balance of payments situation, Fulbright began to emphasize burden-sharing with other industrialized countries and the possibility of more efficient administration of loans by impersonal multilateral financial institutions. Fulbright continued to insist on the depoliticization of the foreign aid program, both through strict separation of military from economic aid, and through removal of the issue from domestic politics via long-term authorization and financing through the Treasury. He did not address himself to the question of how one could mobilize the support of Congress by arguing that economic aid should be depoliticized.

The measures Fulbright believed necessary to put the foreign aid program on a more rational basis were also those strengthening the power of the President. In consonance with his changed beliefs about the proper balance between President and Congress in 1966, he took the lead in changing all aspects of foreign aid authorization which strengthened the President and discovered virtue in dispensing aid through the United Nations.

Fulbright's conception of dissent from prevailing opinion in foreign affairs is intimately connected with the trusteeship model of representation. Faced with oppressive majority opinion, Fulbright believed that the politician would find sustenance in the letter and spirit of the Constitution which is superior to any majority or minority. The politician's oath of office is to uphold the Constitution, not to swing with every breeze of public opinion (1955).

> The oath requires of him . . . [to] reflect the deliberate sense of the community. And this in turn means that he ought to consider himself a teacher. . . . It also means. . . that he must be prepared to accept banishment or destruction at the hands of the people because he has aroused their anger in the very act of serving them well.

While Fulbright's exercises of dissent during the cold war can best be described as agreement on ends but disagreement on means, his dissent since late 1965 appears to be more comprehensive and amounts to offering a new universe of discourse to those who are disenchanted with American foreign policy. The synthesis of ideas apparent in his foreign policy speeches is intended to structure the citizens' perceptions and provide them with the means for reinterpreting the past and responding to present events differently. His rhetoric thus mobilized bias in line with the new assumptions of his operational code (Rosenwasser, 1969).

Perhaps the most striking aspect of Fulbright's rhetoric is that speaking about long-range aspects appears much more congenial to him than busying himself with the details of legislation and oversight. The educator wins out over the lawmaker.

CONCLUSIONS

We described the operational code as the belief portion of Fulbright's decisional premises over a period of twenty-five years. His beliefs were treated as a cluster of variables intervening between independent variables such as political socialization, historical context, political position, and the dependent variable, political behavior. Behavior may have distal social antecedents and may be importantly shaped by the formative political experiences of a person's earlier life. Furthermore, event features of the historical situation do have a great bearing on behavior, and decision-making does not take place in a philosophical atmosphere but rather is a political process.[18] Alternative explanations of some instrumental aspect of Fulbright's behavior are possible in terms of institutional and policy environmental constraints and in terms of the strategic rules informing the decision-making process of Congressional committees. For example, no matter what strategy members of the Senate Foreign Relations Committee adopt—whether policy individualism, bipartisanship, or assertion of institutional independence—the salient environmental feature of foreign policy-making is executive dominance (Fenno, 1973: 187-190).

While the explanatory impulse in political science favors treating cognitive variables as epiphenomena of the situation, we emphasized a cognitive rather than a situational explanation of behavior. The code items we considered are only a portion of the intervening personality processes and dispositions. We intentionally neglected character structure, the deeper functional bases of attitudes, and affective dispositions. What we were interested in were action- or policy-oriented political beliefs, including the ways in which Fulbright defined various roles for himself and his nation. Schematically, the research focus of the paper presents itself as follows:

TABLE 3

FOCUS OF RESEARCH

Independent Variables	Intervening Variables	Dependent Variables
Political Socialization	Personality (character)	
Historical Situation	Policy-oriented Beliefs	Political Behavior
Working Environment	Role Definitions	
	Other Beliefs	
	Attitudes	

Thus, the operational code is only one among other clusters of intervening variables.

The operational code enables an actor to communicate cognitions, ideas, and purposes to significant others in order to mobilize his and their energies and resources towards common political undertakings. Obviously, the significance of the operational code in mobilizing himself and others does not lie in a one-to-one relationship between belief and action; the code does not cause one to do, but it "gives one cause for doing" (Mullins, 1972: 509). The code provides, in other words, grounds or warrants for the political activity engaged in.

In what way, then, can the operational code help us in explaining behavior? We contend, with Leites (1951: 17), that "mere knowledge of . . . rules of conduct does not enable us to predict; but without those rules we would not be able to predict either." To paraphrase an insight from the law, general beliefs do not decide individual policies, for the life of politics is experience. The operational code, therefore, is probably best conceptualized as encouraging or warranting a range of choices, not a specific choice (George, 1969: 200). By identifying the beliefs the actor uses to bound reality, we have an essential tool to predict the range of actions within which his probable choice will be contained and to exclude unlikely ones.

CROSS-SECTIONAL VARIABILITY

First we must be clear about what type of behavior we will analyze. Political actors use different modes of beliefs in different issue areas. In analyzing a legislator, the assumption of issue-related variability adds greatly to explanation. Fulbright's perception of the irrational nature of politics (beliefs 1 and 2) endures in time and cuts across issue contexts. How did Fulbright cope cognitively with irrationality in politics and human nature? Between 1943 and 1965, he had three clusters of cognitive strategies available: in foreign policy, a cluster we might term the rationalist power politics paradigm; in public welfare, a particularist issue politics paradigm; and in race, a "no politics" paradigm.

The rationalist power politics paradigm focuses almost exclusively on the nation-state as the key actor in international politics in general, and on the great powers in particular. Issues are raised by nations only; the dominant issues are war and peace. These issues are resolved through concentration of power in an international organization (1943-45), or through concentration of power in the major nation-states in the form of a balance of power. The cognitive style is highly universalistic, emphasizing general ideas, long-range problems, and neglect of detail. The nation-state is conceived as a unitary rational decision-maker. The status relationship between representative and represented can be described as trusteeship designed to protect the unitary character of the decision maker in foreign policy, the nation-state. Integration into the nation-state system is conditional on performance, demonstrating readiness to delegate power from one unitary actor (nation-state) to another (international organization) if necessary.

In public welfare, the predominant cognitive style is partisanship in a pluralist political culture. The allocation of values involves an incremental process of adjustment in mixed cooperative-conflictual relationships among national political parties, interest groups, and ad hoc coalitions on a multiplicity of issues. The government is not perceived as a unitary actor but a conglomeration of players in the games of public policy. The corresponding model of representation is the politico, forever shaping and adjusting to the various configurations of bargaining. The mode of integration is role participation in the principal institutions engaged in the group process.

In race, the predominant cognitive style is traditionalism, indicating a belief that the problem is insoluble through the political process. Benign inactivity of the government is the decision-making model deemed appropriate, the adjective "benign" referring to Fulbright's belief that education might bring about change in the long run. The model of representation is the instructed delegate humoring the prejudices of his constituency. Integration into the system stresses law and order, with rapid change conceived as destabilizing.

Within each issue context, Fulbright's cognitive style elements and self-definitions have been relatively stable. However, since 1965, there appears to be a distinct tendency in Fulbright to accept the validity of the issue-politics paradigm in all issue contexts. Graphically, we may plot it as follows:

TABLE 4

VALID PARADIGM OF POLITICS

TIME PERIOD	RATIONALIST POWER POLITICS	BUREAUCRATIC ISSUE POLITICS	"NO" POLITICS
1943-1964	Foreign Policy	Public Welfare	Civil Rights
1965 on	⟶ Foreign Policy	Public Welfare	Civil Rights ⟵

An operational code change is indicated by the greater proximity of the civil rights and foreign policy issue contexts to the center paradigm. After 1965, foreign policy increasingly assumes multidimensional characteristics usually associated with domestic public welfare. Peace and war become issues among many others; the multiplicity of issues presumably enables nations to utilize cross-cutting pressures, and a whole spectrum of relations becomes possible, varying in hostility-friendship levels from issue to issue. Similar developments have occurred in the civil rights issue area. Increased participation of blacks in Arkansas politics was bound to affect Fulbright's cognitive strategy in race.

These are very crude generalizations, and refinements are needed in each broad issue context. Quite clearly, in the issue context foreign policy, some areas were closer to domestic politics than others, *vide* foreign economic policy and foreign aid.[19] Yet, despite their crudity, the constructs are helpful in moving discussion of Fulbright's ideology beyond the moralizing which has characterized comment on his race politics and his "neo-isolationism."

LONGITUDINAL VARIABILITY

Once issue context is established, we must assign relative weights to actors in terms of their role in the issue area. Each foreign policy role must be understood as a specialized psychological context. Therefore, we should not expect strict comparability between, let us say, a Secretary of State and a Chairman of the Senate Foreign Relations Committee. In comparing actors performing different roles in the foreign policy process, one expects a higher comparability of the philosophical aspects of the code rather than the instrumental ones, since it is in the realm of the former that the parameters of a nation's foreign policy are set.

Increased comparability necessitates a rank order of operational code items. If some code questions constrain others, and if other researchers discover similarly that some questions are more powerful tappers of codes than others, we will eventually come up with a small number of variables better suited to the task of developing a typology of operational codes. In this respect, incorporating the time dimension in the study proved most fruitful, since identification of one or two code items with great organizing power over a 25-year period increases confidence in their validity.

The most powerful variable in Fulbright's foreign policy operational code was his image of malignant forces in world politics (beliefs 7-11). In 1945, unlimited national sovereignty was the predominant enemy; during 1946-1963, Soviet aggressive totalitarianism was the prime organizer of his code. It was followed by recognition of a limited adversary relationship between the two super-powers, while the totalitarian image of the enemy was retained until 1965 for Asian communism. After that, the principal enemy was the arrogance of the great powers, especially the United States. Graphically, the degree of complexity of the enemy image over time would look as follows:

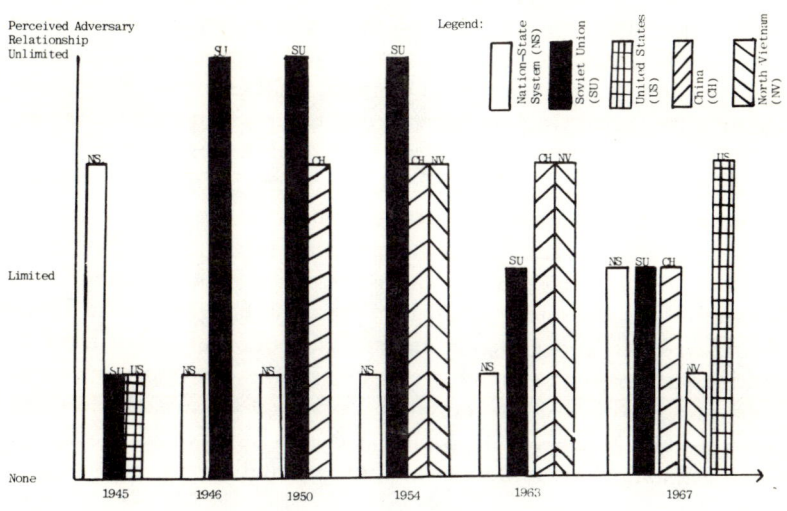

Figure 1: PROFILE OF FULBRIGHT'S IMAGE OF THE ENEMY
Note: Distance between the bars indicates cognitive complexity.

In summary form, the various operational codes of Fulbright appear to be:

Structural Reform Internationalism, 1945

The organizing cognitive tool in 1945 is clearly an antinationalist model. The rules of the game and the patterns of authority characterizing the nation-state system are judged responsible for the recurrence of war (belief 7). Structural reform of the international system will eventually bring about the transfiguration of power politics into world government. With regard to prospects for eventual realization of his antinationalist goal, Fulbright is optimistic, though it is an optimism highly conditional on U.S. performance (belief 16). As for predictability, the image of the enemy clearly entails a belief that we invent our own future through system replacement and social mobilization (beliefs 18 and 19). Control of historical development is influenced by Fulbright's conception of the efficacy of leadership in general (belief 6) and of U.S. leadership in the redemption of history in particular (beliefs 20 and 21). Wars can be avoided through reducing miscalculations of malfeasant leaders (beliefs 23 and 24).

Cognitively associated with these philosophical beliefs is Fulbright's conception of the United States in the role of reformist leader (belief 28). The role of the legislature as protector of the executive in foreign policy from the irrationalities of domestic politics (belief 29) is an important corollary. Goal implementation is consonant with his conception of aggressive leadership; drift is sin (belief 32). Risks are calculated by not becoming a prisoner of blueprints (belief 37), and timing is influenced by the notion that great opportunities arise after great upheavals (belief 40). During this period of reformist leadership, the major United States ends and means are defense of the peace through collective security and gradual transfer of sovereignty to the United Nations, leading to a change in the distribution of power from the nation-state to the community of nations. The charming, but somewhat unsophisticated, community-oriented code was organized by the nation-state system as the principal enemy and predicated upon a high estimate of United States adaptive capability.

Cold War Internationalism, 1946-1963

The organizing cognitive tool during the cold war era is an aggressor-defender model with the Soviet Union cast in the role of aggressor (belief 8) bent upon world conquest, and the United States in the role of defender of Western civilization. Communist doctrine as institutionalized in Soviet aggressive totalitarianism is the main motivating force of Soviet behavior. Monolithicity of communism (excepting Yugoslavia) is taken for granted. The Soviet Union is a unitary actor with a singleness of purpose that calls for similar singleminded purposeful response. Purposefulness is apparent in tight alliance structures under United States leadership (belief 12). Optimism is conditional upon United States performance (belief 16), this time in maintaining the balance of power. In accordance with his strong voluntaristic outlook, he believes that the future is what we make of it through planning (belief 18). He also believes that the Foreign Relations Committee is uniquely qualified to engage in long-range forecasting and that the Executive needs to be shielded from inquiries into the details of foreign policy (belief 29). His belief in the control of historical development is affirmative. The United States has the duty to assume leadership in redeeming history from the scourge of aggressive totalitarianism by organizing countervailing power (beliefs 20 and 21). The role of chance is minimized by making it clear that aggression will be resisted by a preponderance of power (belief 25).

Ironclad alliance commitments will prevent the Communist monolith from advancing.

The power approach also implies that finite resources must not be frittered away but brought to bear in strategic areas (belief 30), and that hopeless goals are not to be pursued indefinitely (belief 33). The most important risk-minimizing rule is avoidance of large-scale commitments on the Asian continent (belief 38). Negotiations must proceed from strength only (belief 41) and nonmilitary foreign policy tools are judged to be more effective than military ones, although the latter are necessary (belief 42). Fulbright's conception of the United States' role is leader of the free world. Control of free world security will be achieved through bypassing the United Nations, balancing the international system, fostering bloc cohesion, transforming the nation-state system at the regional level, and preserving the status quo in the Third World through United States-controlled development.

Limited Adversary Relationship of the United States with the Soviet Union, late 1963 on

By late 1963, the stark cognitive simplicity of the aggressor-defender model gives way to a more differentiated model of a mixed-cooperative conflict relationship between the superpowers. Fulbright's threat perception has clearly changed. The mechanist presumption of monolithicity is gone. The image of the enemy is no longer a relentless aggressive totalitarianism on the march, to be contained by vigorous countermeasures. Doctrine is no longer considered the prime mover of Soviet foreign policy. Communist decision makers can no longer be predicted by simply knowing the scriptures of Marxism-Leninism. Moscow is still a unitary purposive actor, but acts much like other great powers in response to the opportunities and strictures of the international system.

The simplicity of the aggressor-defender model is still apparent in Fulbright's assessment of "Asian communism." The ways to influence Chinese and North Vietnamese behavior are still the ways of containment as long as Asian communist perspectives of the outside world are distorted by assumptions of implacable United States hostility.

Preservative Internationalism, 1966 on

By early 1966, Fulbright identified as the major enemy the arrogance of great nations in general, and of the United States specifical-

TABLE 5

FULBRIGHT'S THREE OPERATIONAL CODES

Time Period	Image of Dominant Enemy	U.S. National Role	Principal End	Principal Means	Necessity of Presidential Domination	Role of Legislature	Estimate of Adaptive Capability	Sector Favored for Resource Allocation
1945 Structural Reform Internationalism	Nation-State System	Reformist Leader	System Transformation	Gradual Build-up of the United Nations	High	Restricted	High	Foreign
1946-1963 Cold War Internationalism	Soviet Aggressive Totalitarianism	Free World Leader	System Control Through Balance of Power	Collective Defense, Regional Transformation, Development of the Third World	High	Restricted	High	Foreign
1966 Preservative Internationalism	Arrogance of Power	Low Posture Leader	Civilizing Nation-State System Through Example	Multilateral Functional Enterprises, Domestic Reconstruction	Low	Active	Low	Domestic

ly. From the leadership of Western consolidationist actions against Communist expansion, he sees the United States moving into the category of expansionist powers itself (belief 11). Increased questioning of the nation-state system as a useful authority structure indicates a revival of the antinationalist model. Functionalism assumes an ever-increasing importance. Alliance structures must be loosened (belief 13). International education, always a potent benign force, gains even greater saliency (belief 15). Fulbright's confidence in the future loses much of its exuberance (belief 17). As for prediction, no longer is the problem so much one of long-range forecasting but of warning against the more specific short-range policies of a particular President. Pessimistic capability judgments find expression in the discovery of the power of example as a potent redemptive force in history (belief 22). This is still a leadership posture, but obviously a very low-key one. Misperception is now the primary cause of war and conflict (belief 27). Historical analogies must be discarded. Awareness of the danger of black-and-white thinking, the function of diabolical enemy-images, and the self-fulfilling prophecy will usher in a period of empathy and understanding.

The low posture role conception Fulbright discovers as appropriate for the United States (belief 31) consists primarily of United States attempts to civilize the nation-state system through functionalist enterprises. Presidential-Congressional relations must be based on institutional rather than precarious personal judgments (belief 36). The risks of executive dominance in foreign affairs will be checked by a strong legislature (belief 39). The primary purpose of dissent is the creation of a new universe of discourse in American foreign policy (belief 44). Fulbright's three operational codes can be presented schematically, as at left.

We discovered two great cleavages in Fulbright's operational code —1946 and 1966—both associated with changes in the image of the dominant enemy.[20] These changes seem to be associated with changes in United States role conceptions and Presidential-Congressional relations. Next in importance are estimates of adaptive capability, another term for control of historical development. High capability judgments incline a political actor towards system transformation and system control. Estimates of adaptive capabilities in turn are intimately related to judgments about which sector—foreign or domestic —should be favored for resource allocation.

These are, of course, qualitative judgments; the question is, to what extent are these code items accessible to operationalization? Some appear to be open to analysis of roll call votes in the case of legislators, others to a variant of quantitative content analysis.[21] However, it should not be forgotten that decision makers themselves tend to deal with these variables in qualitative and sometimes incredibly imprecise terms, and the greater precision introduced by the analyst through quantitative techniques may not necessarily result in greater predictive power (George et al., 1971: 257). Furthermore, the explanatory power of the qualitative model represented by our table (which is really a series of hypotheses or hunches) appears quite satisfactory as it stands now. There is hardly a vote cast by Fulbright that could not be retrodicted by the operational code. The real problem is not whether qualitative or quantitative analysis is more fruitful, but whether qualitative analysis of the kind undertaken here is parsimonious. It is a question which the author, for obvious reasons, declines to answer.

We believe this paper demonstrates the importance of incorporating more systematically the time dimension into the operational code construct. While actors need stabilized images—whether of self, others, or significant environments—in order to function, one should beware of the tendency to overestimate the unity of personality in the life-history of the individual. For predictive purposes, a number of interesting questions need answering. What is the minimum time period within which operational codes may be considered stable? Do rates of change differ according to actor roles? What are the temporal differences in the relative strength among different components of the operational code? Some of these questions obviously cannot be answered even tentatively without considering variables other than the operational code, especially the field in which behavior occurs.

Our focus in this paper has been directed towards a limited but we think important segment of Fulbright's decisional premises. We did not try to establish whether he was morally wrong or right, now or then. We tried to understand Fulbright's behavior rather than to assign blame and guilt. We do think, though, that the Senator is an instructive example of the melancholy truth that of all the constraints pressing upon a political actor, the inner constraints in the form of beliefs may be the most stifling.

NOTES

1. Brim et al. (1962: 234-235) have experimentally validated that general epistemological beliefs influence problem-solving indirectly through instrumental beliefs.

2. Assumptions that actors need a cognitive framework to know and understand "reality," use beliefs to express what they consider to be facts, and engage in a screening process to select out the properties relevant to a particular choice, mesh with important psychological postulates underlying a main body of organization theory (March and Simon, 1958; Braybrooke and Lindblom, 1963).

3. For forceful statements on the blessing and curse of interdependence of facts and theories, see Jervis (1968, 1972) and Lindblom (1968: 23).

4. Fishbein and Rowen (1962: 42) suggest defining belief as the probability dimension of a concept and attitude as the evaluative dimension. Similarly, Milbrath (1966: 45), differentiates between values and attitudes as cognitions with attached valences on the one hand, and belief as a cognition to which credulity is attached.

5. For two fine discussions of multiple meanings of these terms, see Mullins (1972) and Cobb (1973).

6. For a comprehensive bibliography covering the period up to 1967, see Tweraser (1971); for one dealing with a specific issue-area, see Perry (1968). The Senator's most recent book, The Crippled Giant (1972), was included in the analysis. The author has also cautiously relied upon various biographies and biographical articles; the best available of the genre is still: Fulbright, The Dissenter (Johnson and Gwertzman, 1968).

7. For a complex discussion of inferential problems, see George (1959a and b); for a related treatment, see Hoffmann (1969).

8. See K. J. Holsti's (1970) suggestive discussion of national role conceptions in the study of foreign policy.

9. The latter speech was significantly titled "A Creative War"—Fulbright's version of the just war, justified as long as it held out the possibility of a transformation of the international system through international government.

10. Evidence for Fulbright's belief (1946a: 50) in the immoral nature of Communism can be adduced from the following:

> It is the religion of the state, of the party, the pagan principle that the individual is nothing and the party everything, that is the real danger to our Western Christian civilization. If . . . Russia is interested simply in a higher standard of living and security for her people, there is little cause for alarm, but if she is intent upon saving our souls, there can be no limit to her aggression or to her ruthlessness.

A representative indication of his view of Fascism is the statement (Northwest Arkansas Times, 1944): "The essence of Fascism is the denial of the integrity and dignity of the individual human being. It is the belief that brute force and power is good in itself, and that justice is a silly dream."

11. There is experimental evidence (Greenwell and Dengerink, 1973: 66-71) that symbolic attack, or specifically the perceived aggressive intent of the attacker, appears to be a more potent instigator of vigorous counter-measures than physical attack per se. The above seems to be a more helpful explanation of Fulbright's image change than the hypothesis (Gladstone, 1959: 132-137) that projection is the defense mechanism which is most relevant for understanding the conception of the enemy.

12. Fulbright's belief in the beneficial function of education is one of the constants of

his operational code, cutting across issue-contexts. In the issue-context of race, it is education that will ultimately improve relations between blacks and whites. Racial peace will come through consensus, not governmental action.

13. For a suggestive discussion of forecasting in terms of social purposes, see Bobrow, 1973.

14. Adaptive capability is an estimate of those natural, material, human, and institutional resources of the nation-state that comprise its potential over an extended period of time for coping with present and foreseeable demands from the geopolitical environment, and for exerting a measure of control over it (Lovell, 1970: 146). Power, as used in this paper, is an existential proposition regarding one's belief about his own or his nation's relative capacity to influence and/or control the structure and operation of the environment.

15. By 1969, Fulbright (U.S. Congress, 1969: 13056) showed signs of doubt about the efficacy of the American example:

> Perhaps it was vanity, but we supposed that we could be an example for the world . . . an example of rationality and restraint. We supposed, as Woodrow Wilson put it, that a rational world order could be created embodying not a balance of power but a community of power, not organized rivalries, but an organized common peace.

16. In fairness to Fulbright, it should be pointed out that his role conception was widely shared by political scientists. Fenno (1964: 674) criticized the belief in the beneficence of Presidential supremacy with the following:

> to relegate Congress to the making of broad policy decisions . . . is to prescribe precisely those tasks which Congress is least capable of performing. To criticize Congress for intervening in a specific and detailed fashion is to attack it for doing the only thing it can do to assert its influence. Specifics and details are the indispensable handles which Congressmen use to work intuitively toward broader kinds of oversight judgments.

17. Fulbright has been on the Joint Economic Committee since 1953. For a description of this committee, see Huitt (1963: 478-479).

18. For a detailed schematic map suitable for the analysis of personality and politics, see Smith (1968: 25).

19. For a recent attempt to develop an issue area framework in foreign policy, see Zimmerman (1973).

20. The period of 1943-1965 roughly coincides with what Rosenau (1970) has called a foreign policy of promotive adaptation, whereas the 1966 stance resembles the policy of preservative adaptation.

21. For suggestive ways of operationalizing perceptions and images of decision makers, see, for example, Choucri (1969) and Brecher, Steinberg, and Stein (1969).

REFERENCES

EXPLANATORY NOTE: The following system was used to reference primary materials: Under "Fulbright" are listed all his books and articles, speeches available in mimeographed form from his speech files, and letters available in the James William Fulbright Papers at the University of Arkansas Library, Fayetteville; under "U.S. Congress" are listed his remarks on the floor and his speeches inserted in the Congressional Record; and under different Senate Committees, his remarks in public committee sessions.

ALLISON, G. T. (1971) Essence of Decision: Explaining the Cuban Missile Crisis. Boston: Little, Brown.
────── and H. M. HALPERIN (1972) "Bureaucratic politics: a paradigm and some policy implications." World Politics 24 (Spring), Supplement: 40-79.
ANDERSON, J. E. (1973) "The 'operational code' approach: the George construct and Senator A. Vandenberg's operational code belief system." Paper presented at Annual Meeting, Amer. Pol. Sci. Assn., New Orleans.
Arkansas Democrat (1951) January 31.
Arkansas Gazette (1955) August 25.
────── (1954) April 18.
────── (1953) September 16.
────── (1951a) January 31.
────── (1951b) July 16.
────── (1949a) May 29.
────── (1949b) February 20.
────── (1946) September 8.
ASHBY, N. (1970) "Schumacher and Brandt: the divergent operational codes of two German socialist leaders." Paper prepared for Seminar in Political Leadership, Stanford University.
AXELROD, R. (1973) "Schema theory: an information processing model of perception and cognition." Amer. Pol. Sci. Rev. 67 (December): 1248-1266.
BARBER, J. D. (1968) "Classifying and predicting presidential styles: two 'weak' presidents." J. of Social Issues 24 (July): 51-80.
BARNET, J. R. (1971) The Roots of War: The Men and Institutions behind U.S. Foreign Policy. Baltimore: Penguin Books.
BOBROW, D. B. (1973) "Criteria for valid forecasting." Presented at International Relationship Forecasting Conference, M.I.T., Cambridge.
BRECHER, M., B. STEINBERG, and J. STEIN (1969) "A framework for research on foreign policy behavior." J. of Conflict Resolution 13 (March): 75-101.
BRIM, O. G., D. C. GLASS, D. E. LAVIN, N. GOODMAN (1962) Personality and Decision Process. Stanford: Stanford University Press.
CHOUCRI, N. (1969) "The perceptual base of non-alignment." J. of Conflict Resolution 13 (March): 57-74.
CLAUSEN, A. R. (1973) How Congressmen Decide: A Policy Focus. New York: St. Martin's.
COBB, R. W. (1973) "The belief-systems perspective: an assessment of a framework." J. of Politics 35 (February): 121-153.
CONGRESSIONAL QUARTERLY ALMANAC (1967) 23: 312-313.
DEXTER, L. A. (1956) "What do Congressmen hear: the mail." Public Opinion Quarterly 20 (Spring): 16-27.
DOWNS, C. W. (1963) "A thematic analysis of speeches on foreign policy of Senator J. W. Fulbright." Ph. D. dissertation, Michigan State University.
EULAU, H. (1967) "Changing views of representation," in I. de Sola Pool (ed.) Contemporary Political Science: Toward Empirical Theory. New York: McGraw-Hill.
FENNO, R. F. (1973) Congressmen in Committees. Boston: Little, Brown.

―――― (1964) "Book review of Joseph P. Harris' Congressional Control of Administration." Amer. Pol. Sci. Rev. 58 (September): 673-674.
FINNEY, J. W. (1971) "Foreign Policy: Congress more active." New York Times (January 23): 1, 8.
FISHBEIN, M. and B. H. ROWEN (1962) "The AB scales: an operational definition of belief and attitudes." Human Relations 15 (February): 35-44.
FULBRIGHT, J. W. (1972) Crippled Giant: American Foreign Policy and Its Domestic Consequences. New York: Vintage Books.
―――― (1968a) "Elite and electorate." The Center Magazine 1 (November): 64-65.
―――― (1968b) "For a new order of priorities at home and abroad." Playboy 15 (July): 110-111, 116, 152-157.
―――― (1967a) "Human nature and the cold war." Presented at Wilmington College, Ohio.
―――― (1967b) "The great society is a sick society." New York Times Magazine (August 20): 30-31.
―――― (1967c) "Why are we fighting in Vietnam?" Presented at the Stephens College Lecture Series on International Affairs, Columbia, Mo.
―――― (1966a) The Arrogance of Power. New York: Random House.
―――― (1966b) "Education for a new kind of international relations." Presented at Annual Meeting of the Swedish Institute for Cultural Relations, Stockholm.
―――― (1966c) The Vietnam Hearings. New York: Vintage Press.
―――― (1965a) Speech presented at Consultative Assembly of the Council of Europe, Strasbourg, France.
―――― (1965b) Meet the Press Interview, March 14. Washington: Merkle Press.
―――― (1965c) "Approaches to international community." Presented at Pennsylvania State University, University Park.
―――― (1964a) Old Myths and New Realities. New York: Random House.
―――― (1964b) "The cold war in American life." Presented at Univ. of North Carolina, Chapel Hill.
―――― (1963a) "Is government by the people possible?" Presented at The Fund for the Republic, Inc., New York.
―――― (1963b) Prospects for the West. Cambridge: Harvard Univ. Press.
―――― (1962) Speech presented at Italian Soc. for International Organization, Rome.
―――― (1961a) "American foreign policy in the 20th century under an 18th century constitution." Cornell Law Quarterly 47 (Fall): 1-13.
―――― (1961b) "For a concert of free nations." Foreign Affairs 40 (October): 1-18.
―――― (1959) "Our responsibility in world affairs: the role of the Senate." Vital Speeches 25 (June): 527-532.
―――― (1955) "The mummification of opinion." Presented at Annual National Book Award Dinner, New York.
―――― (1954a) "Bipartisanship is a two-way street." Reporter 11 (December): 8-11.
―――― (1954b) Letter to Ben V. Cohen, December 23.
―――― (1953-1954) "Julian S. Waterman—a memorial." Arkansas Law Rev. and Bar Assn. Journal 8: 64-66.
―――― (1953a) Letter to B. L. McCullogh, February 13.
―――― (1953b) Letter to William Esslinger, March 7.
―――― (1952) Letter to B. A. Rogers, June 19.
―――― (1951a) "Congressional investigations: significance for the legislative process." University of Chicago Law Rev. 18: 440-448.
―――― (1951b) Letter to Mrs. George Burris and Mrs. T. S. Daniel, May 15.

——— (1951c) Letter to William H. Springston, May 18.
——— (1950a) Letter to John E. Wells, June 22.
——— (1950b) Letter to Ken Johnson, November 24.
——— (1949) Letter to James G. Daly, June 4.
——— (1948a) The New World Looks at the Old. Toronto: Univ. of Toronto Press.
——— (1948b) "A United States of Europe?" Annals of Amer. Academy of Pol. and Soc. Sciences 257 (May): 151-156.
——— (1948c) Letter to Allen W. Dulles, July 17.
——— (1947a) Letter to Eleanor Neill, April 2.
——— (1947b) Letter to George C. Collier, March 27.
——— (1947c) Letter to Herbert E. Gaston, October 28.
——— (1946a) "Is it the purpose of Russia to dominate the world?" in K. E. Meyer (ed.) Fulbright of Arkansas: The Public Positions of a Private Thinker. Washington: Robert B. Luce, Inc.
——— (1946b) "If Congress is bad, then so is the voter." New York Times Magazine (November 3): 7, 65-66.
——— (1945a) "Sovereignty and the charter." New Republic 113 (August): 158-159.
——— (1945b) Letter to August Engel, December 19.
——— (1945c) Letter to Lt. Cdr. Bernal Seamster, May 26.
——— (1945d) Letter to Edward J. Meeman, March 19.
——— (1945e) Letter to Benjamin B. Wallace, March 16.
——— (1945f) Letter to William R. Shaw, October 9.
——— (1945g) Letter to S/Sgt. Robert Hobson, November 6.
——— (1943) "Congress and peace." J. of the Natl. Educ. Assn. 32 (November): 217-218.
——— (1942) Letter to Edwin W. Pauley, November 23.
——— (1939) "The social function of the University." Presented at Fort Smith, Ark.
GEORGE, A. L. (1974) "Assessing presidential character." World Politics 26 (January): 234-282.
——— (1972) "The case for multiple advocacy in making foreign policy." Amer. Pol. Sci. Rev. 66 (September): 751-785.
——— D. K. HALL and W. R. SIMONS (1971) The Limits of Coercive Diplomacy: Laos, Cuba, Vietnam. Boston: Little, Brown.
——— (1969) "The 'operational code': a neglected approach to the study of political leaders and decision making." Internat. Studies Quarterly 13 (June): 190-222.
——— (1959a) Propaganda Analysis: A Study of Inference Made from Nazi Propaganda in World War II. Evanston: Row, Peterson.
——— (1959b) "Quantitative and qualitative approaches to content analysis," in I. de Sola Pool (ed.) Trends in Content Analysis. Urbana: Univ. of Illinois Press.
GLAD, B. (1973) "Contributions of psycho-biology," in J. N. Knutson (ed.) Handbook of Political Psychology. San Francisco: Jossey-Bass.
——— (1969) "The significance of personality for role performance as Chairman of the Senate Foreign Relations Committee: a comparison of Borah and Fulbright." Presented at annual meeting, Amer. Pol. Sci. Assn., New York.
GLADSTONE, A. (1959) "The conception of the enemy." J. of Conflict Resolution 3 (June): 132-137.
GLENN, E. S. (1966) "A cognitive approach to the analysis of cultures and cultural evolution," in L. von Bertahlanffy and A. Rapoport (eds.) General Systems: Yearbook of the Society for General Systems Research 9. Ann Arbor: Soc. for General Systems Research: 115-132.

GREENWELL, J. and H. A. DENGERINK (1973) "The role of perceived versus actual attack in human physical aggression." J. of Personality and Social Psychology 26 (April): 66-71.

GUHIN, M. A. (1972) John Foster Dulles: A Statesman and His Times. New York: Columbia Univ. Press.

GUTIERREZ, G. G. (1973) "Dean Rusk and Southeast Asia: an operational code analysis." Presented at annual meeting, Amer. Pol. Sci. Assn., New Orleans.

HALPERIN, M. (1960) "Is the Senate's foreign relations research worthwhile?" Amer. Behavioral Scientist 4 (September): 21-24.

HOFFMAN, E. P. (1969) "Methodological problems of Kreminology," In F. J. Fleron (ed.) Communist Studies and the Social Sciences: Essays on Methodology and Empirical Theory. Chicago: Rand McNally.

HOLSTI, K. J. (1972) International Politics: A Framework for Analysis. Englewood Cliffs: Prentice-Hall.

——— (1970) "National role conceptions in the study of foreign policy." Internat. Studies Quarterly 14 (November): 233-309.

HOLSTI, O. (1970) "The 'operational code' approach to the study of political leaders: John Foster Dulles' philosophical and instrumental beliefs." Canadian J. of Pol. Sci. 3 (March): 123-157.

HUITT, R. K. (1963) "Congressional organization and operation in the field of money and credit," in W. Fellner, R. A. Musgrave, J. Tobin, J. R. Schlesinger, P. H. Cootner, I. Auerbach, R. K. Huitt, J. Lindeman. Fiscal and Debt Management Policies. Englewood Cliffs: Prentice-Hall.

——— (1954) "The congressional committee: a case study." Amer. Pol. Sci. Rev. 48 (June): 340-365.

——— and R. L. PEABODY (1969) Congress: Two Decades of Analysis. New York: Harper & Row.

HYMAN, S. (1959) "The advice and consent of J. William Fulbright." Reporter 21 (September 20): 23-25.

JERVIS, R. (1972) "Consistency in foreign policy views," in R. L. Merritt (ed.) Communication in International Politics. Urbana: Univ. of Illinois Press.

——— (1970) The Logic of Images in International Relations. Princeton: Princeton Univ. Press.

——— (1968) "Hypotheses on misperceptions." World Politics 20 (April): 454-479.

JOHNSON, H. and GWERTZMAN, B. (1968) Fulbright: The Dissenter. Garden City: Doubleday.

JOHNSON, L. (1973) "Operational codes and the prediction of leadership behavior: Senator Frank Church at mid-career." Presented at annual meeting, Amer. Pol. Sci. Assn., New Orleans.

JOHNSON, W. and F. J. COLLIGAN (1965) The Fulbright Program: A History. Chicago: Univ. of Chicago Press.

KALLEBERG, A. L. (1969) "Concept formation in normative and empirical studies: toward reconciliation in political theory." Amer. Pol. Sci. Rev. 63 (March): 26-39.

KAVANAGH, D. (1971) "The 'operational code' of Ramsay MacDonald." Unpublished paper, Stanford Univ.

KELMAN, H. C. (1969) "Patterns of personal involvement in the national system: a social-psychological analysis of political legitimacy," in J. N. Rosenau (ed.) International Politics and Foreign Policy: A Reader in Research and Theory. New York: Free Press.

KENWORTHY, E. W. (1959) "The Fulbright idea of foreign policy," New York Times

Magazine (May 10): 10-11, 74-78.
LEITES, N. (1953) A Study of Bolshevism. Glencoe: Free Press.
—— (1951) Operational Code of the Politburo. New York: McGraw-Hill.
LEVI, W. (1970) "Ideology, interests, and foreign policy." Internat. Studies Quarterly 14 (March): 1-31.
LINDBLOM, C. (1968) The Policy-Making Process. Englewood Cliffs: Prentice-Hall.
LOVELL, J. P. (1970) Foreign Policy in Perspective; Strategy, Adaptation, Decision Making. New York: Holt, Rinehart and Winston.
MANTEL, H. N. (1959) "The Congressional Record: Fact or fiction of the legislative process." Western Pol. Quarterly 12 (December): 981-995.
MARCH, J. and H. A. SIMON (1958) Organizations. New York: Wiley.
MCFARLAND, A. S. (1969) Power and Leadership in Pluralist Systems. Stanford: Stanford Univ. Press.
MCLELLAN, D. S. (1971) "The 'operational code' approach to the study of political leaders: Dean Acheson's philosophical and instrumental beliefs." Canadian J. of Pol. Sci. 4 (March): 52-75.
MEYER, K. (1963) [ed.] Fulbright of Arkansas. The Public Positions of a Private Thinker. Washington: Robert B. Luce, Inc.
MILBRATH, L. (1966) "Beliefs: a neglected unit of analysis in comparative politics," in E. L. Finney (ed.) Comparative Politics and Political Theory. Durham: Univ. of N. Carolina Press.
MORROW, W. L. (1969) Congressional Committees. New York: Charles Scribner.
MULLINS, W. A. (1972) "On the concept of ideology in political science." Amer. Pol. Sci. Rev. 66 (June): 498-510.
NORTH, R. C., O. R. HOLSTI, M. G. ZANINOVICH, and D. A. ZINNES (1963) Content Analysis: A Handbook with Applications for the Study of International Crisis. Evanston: Northwestern Univ. Press.
Northwest Arkansas Times (1949) August 1.
—— (1948a) November 3.
—— (1948b) September 25.
—— (1947a) April 14.
—— (1947b) April 15.
—— (1946a) September 19.
—— (1946b) October 1.
—— (1945) March 5.
—— (1944) September 29.
PERRY, B. (1968) "Senator J. William Fulbright on European and Atlantic Unity." Ph.D. dissertation, Univ. of Pennsylvania.
PRUITT, D. G. and J. P. GAHAGAN (1972) "Campus crisis: the search for power." Unpublished manuscript. Buffalo: State Univ. of New York.
PUTMAN, R. D. (1971) "Studying elite political culture: the case of 'ideology'." Amer. Pol. Sci. Rev. 65 (September): 651-681.
ROBINSON, J. A. (1960) "Another look at the Senate research on foreign policy." Amer. Behavioral Scientist 4 (November): 12-14.
ROSENAU, J. N. (1970) The Adaptation of National Societies: A Theory of Political Systems Behavior and Transformation. New York: McCaleb-Seiler.
—— (1959) "Senate attitudes toward a Secretary of State," J. C. Wahlke and H. Eulau (eds.) Legislative Behavior. New York: Free Press.
ROSENWASSER, M. E. J. (1969) "Six Senate war critics and their appeals for gaining audience response." Today's Speech 17 (September): 43-50.

SENATE COMMITTEE ON ARMED SERVICES and COMMITTEE ON FOREIGN RELATIONS (1951) Hearings on Military Situation in the Far East.
SENATE COMMITTEE ON FOREIGN RELATIONS (1966) Hearings on United States Policy toward Europe and Related Matters.
—— (1961) Hearings on International Development and Security.
—— (1960) Hearings on United States Foreign Policy.
—— (1959) Hearings on Inter-American Development Bank Act.
—— (1949a) Hearings on Extension of European Recovery.
—— (1949b) Hearings on North Atlantic Treaty.
—— and SENATE COMMITTEE ON ARMED SERVICES (1957) Hearings on the President's Proposal on the Middle East.
SENATE COMMITTEE ON THE JUDICIARY, SUBCOMMITTEE ON SEPARATION OF POWERS (1967) Hearings on Separation of Powers.
SENATE SPECIAL COMMITTEE TO STUDY THE FOREIGN AID PROGRAM (1957) Hearings on the Foreign Aid Program.
SIMON, H. A. (1957a) Administrative Behavior. New York: Macmillan.
—— (1957b) Models of Man. New York: Wiley.
SINGER, J. D. (1968) "Man and world politics: the Psycho-cultural interface." J. of Social Issues 24 (July): 127-156.
—— (1964) "Soviet and American foreign policy attitudes: content analysis of elite articulation." J. of Conflict Resolution 8 (December): 424-485.
SMITH, M. B. (1968) "A map for the analysis of personality and politics." J. of Social Issues 24 (July): 15-28.
STASSEN, G. H. (1972) "Individual preference versus role-constraint in policy-making: Senatorial response to Secretaries Acheson and Dulles." World Politics 25 (October): 96-119.
STUPAK, R. (1969) The Shaping of Foreign Policy: The Role of the Secretary of State as Seen by Dean Acheson. Indianapolis: Odyssey Press.
TILLEMA, H. K. (1973) Appeal to Force: American Military Intervention in the Era of Containment. New York: Crowell.
TWERASER, K. K. (1971) "The advice and dissent of Senator Fulbright: a longitudinal analysis of his images of international politics and his political role conceptions." Ph.D. dissertation, The American Univ.
U.S. Congress, Congressional Record (1969) May 20.
—— (1967) March 16.
—— (1966a) February 2.
—— (1966b) July 18, July 26.
—— (1966c) January 14.
—— (1965a) September 15.
—— (1965b) October 22.
—— (1964a) August 6.
—— (1964b) August 6.
—— (1964c) August 7.
—— (1964d) June 23.
—— (1963a) August 2.
—— (1963b) January 24.
—— (1961a) July 24.
—— (1961b) July 29.
—— (1961c) July 29.
—— (1959a) April 16.

——— (1959b) April 16.
——— (1959c) July 15.
——— (1958a) August 27.
——— (1958b) June 20.
——— (1957) February 20.
——— (1956a) February 27.
——— (1956b) February 27.
——— (1954) February 2.
——— (1951a) March 27.
——— (1951b) January 22.
——— (1951c) January 5.
——— (1951d) January 22.
——— (1951e) January 22.
——— (1951f) August 30.
——— (1949) March 30, July 15.
——— (1948) August 6.
——— (1947a) April 7.
——— (1947b) April 7.
——— (1947c) April 7.
——— (1947d) January 15.
——— (1946a) February 19.
——— (1946b) July 29.
——— (1945a) July 9.
——— (1945b) March 28.
——— (1945c) July 27-28.
——— (1945d) November 26.
——— (1945e) March 12.
——— (1945f) July 18.
——— (1945g) July 19.
——— (1945h) March 28.
——— (1945i) July 23.
——— (1945j) October 29.
——— (1945k) January 6.
——— (1945l) January 15.
——— (1945m) July 9.
——— (1944a) January 26.
——— (1944b) January 21.
——— (1943a) May 13.
——— (1943b) March 15.
——— (1943c) February 8.
——— (1943d) February 16.
VERBA, S. (1965) "Conclusion: comparative political culture," in S. Verba and L. Pye (eds.) Political Culture and Political Development. Princeton: Princeton Univ. Press.
——— (1961) "Assumptions of rationality and non-rationality in models of the international system," in K. Knorr and S. Verba (eds.) The International System: Theoretical Essays. Princeton: Princeton Univ. Press.
WAHLKE, J. C., H. ELAU, W. BUCHANAN, L. C. FERGUSON (1962) The Legislative System: Explorations in Legislative Behavior. New York: Wiley.
WALTZ, K. N. (1965) "Contention and management in international relations." World Politics 17 (July): 720-744.

WHITE, D. G. (1970) "A comparison of the operational code of Mao Tse-Tung and Liu Shao-Ch'i." Paper prepared for Center for East Asian Studies, Stanford Univ.

WICKER, A. L. (1969) "Attitudes versus actions: the relationship of verbal and overt behavioral responses to attitude objects." J. of Social Issues 25 (Autumn): 41-78.

ZIMMERMAN, W. (1973) "Issue area and foreign-policy process: a research note in search of a general theory." Amer. Pol. Sci. Rev. 67 (December): 1204-1212.

A Better Way of Getting New Information

Research, survey and policy studies that say what needs to be said—no more, no less.

The Sage Papers Program

Eight regularly-issued original paperback series that bring, at an unusually low cost, the timely writings and findings of the international scholarly community. Since the material is updated on a continuing basis, each series rapidly becomes a unique repository of vital information.

Authoritative, and frequently seminal, works that NEED to be available

- To scholars and practitioners
- In university and institutional libraries
- In departmental collections
- For classroom adoption

Sage Professional Papers
COMPARATIVE POLITICS SERIES
INTERNATIONAL STUDIES SERIES
ADMINISTRATIVE AND POLICY STUDIES SERIES
AMERICAN POLITICS SERIES
CONTEMPORARY POLITICAL SOCIOLOGY SERIES
POLITICAL ECONOMY SERIES

Sage Policy Papers
THE WASHINGTON PAPERS

Sage Research Papers

SAGE PUBLICATIONS
The Publishers of Professional Social Science
Beverly Hills • London

Sage Professional Papers in Comparative Politics

Editors: Aristide R. Zolberg, *University of Chicago*
Richard Merritt, *University of Illinois*

(Volumes I thru IV edited by Harry Eckstein and Ted Robert Gurr)

VOLUME I (1970)

01-001	J. Z. Namenwirth and H. D. Lasswell, The Changing Language of American Values: A Computer Study of Selected Party Platforms (72 pp)	$2.50
01-002	K. Janda, A Conceptual Framework for the Comparative Analysis of Political Parties (56 pp)	$1.90
01-003	K. Thompson, Cross-national Voting Behavior Research: An Example of Computer-Assisted Multivariate Analysis of Attribute Data (48 pp)	$1.50
01-004	W. B. Quandt, The Comparative Study of Political Elites (64 pp)	$2.00
01-005	M. C. Hudson, Conditions of Political Violence and Instability: A Preliminary Test of Three Hypotheses (56 pp)	$1.90
01-006	E. Ozbudun, Party Cohesion in Western Democracies: A Causal Analysis (96 pp)	$3.00
01-007	J. R. Nellis, A Model of Developmental Ideology in Africa: Structure and Implications (40 pp)	$1.40
01-008	A. Kornberg, et al., Semi-Careers in Political Work: The Dilemma of Party Organizations (40 pp)	$1.40
01-009	F. I. Greenstein and S. Tarrow, Political Orientations of Children: The Use of a Semi-Projective Technique in Three Nations (88 pp)	$2.90
01-010	F. W. Riggs, Administrative Reform and Political Responsiveness: A Theory of Dynamic Balance (48 pp)	$1.50
01-011	R. H. Donaldson and D. J. Waller, Stasis and Change in Revolutionary Elites: A Comparative Analysis of the 1956 Central Party Committees in China and the USSR (56 pp)	$1.90
01-012	R. A. Pride, Origins of Democracy: A Cross-National Study of Mobilization, Party Systems, and Democratic Stability (88 pp)	$2.90

VOLUME II (1971)

01-013	S. Verba, et al., The Modes of Democratic Participation: A Cross-National Comparison (80 pp)	$2.80
01-014	W. R. Schonfeld, Youth and Authority in France: A Study of Secondary Schools (80 pp)	$2.80
01-015	S. J. Bodenheimer, The Ideology of Developmentalism: The American Paradigm-Surrogate for Latin American Studies (56 pp)	$2.40
01-016	L. Sigelman, Modernization and the Political System: A Critique and Preliminary Empirical Analysis (64 pp)	$2.50
01-017	H. Eckstein, The Evaluation of Political Performance: Problems and Dimensions (88 pp)	$2.90
01-018	T. Gurr and M. McClelland, Political Performance: A Twelve-Nation Study (88 pp)	$2.90
01-019	R. F. Moy, A Computer Simulation of Democratic Political Development: Tests of the Lipset and Moore Models (72 pp)	$2.70
01-020	T. Nardin, Violence and the State: A Critique of Empirical Political Theory (72 pp)	$2.70
01-021	W. Ilchman, Comparative Public Administration and "Conventional Wisdom" (56 pp)	$2.40
01-022	G. Bertsch, Nation-Building in Yugoslavia: A Study of Political Integration and Attitudinal Consensus (48 pp)	$2.25
01-023	R. J. Willey, Democracy in West German Trade Unions: A Reappraisal of the "Iron Law" (56 pp)	
01-024	R. Rogowski and L. Wasserspring, Does Political Development Exist? Corporatism in Old and New Societies (56 pp)	

VOLUME III (1972)

01-025	W. T. Daly, The Revolutionary: A Review and Synthesis (40 pp)
01-026	C. Stone, Stratification and Political Change in Trinidad and Jamaica (40 pp)
01-027	Z. Y. Gitelman, The Diffusion of Political Innovation: From Eastern Europe to the Soviet Union (64 pp)
01-028	D. P. Conradt, The West German Party System: An Ecological Analysis of Social Structure and Voting Behavior, 1961-1969 (56 pp)
01-029	J. R. Scarritt, Political Development and Culture Change Theory: A Propositional Synthesis with Application to Africa (64 pp)
01-030	M. D. Hayes, Policy Outputs in the Brazilian States, 1940-1960: Political and Economic Correlates (48 pp)
01-031	B. Stallings, Economic Dependency in Africa and Latin America (64 pp)
01-032	J. T. Campos and J. F. McCamant, Cleavage Shift in Colombia: Analysis of the 1970 Elections (84 pp)
01-033	G. Field and J. Higley, Elites in Developed Societies: Theoretical Reflections on an Initial Stage in Norway (48 pp)
01-034	J. S. Szyliowicz, A Political Analysis of Student Activism: The Turkish Case (80 pp)
01-035	E. C. Hargrove, Professional Roles in Society and Government: The English Case (88 pp)
01-036	A. J. Sofranko and R. C. Bealer, Unbalanced Modernization and Domestic Instability: A Comparative Analysis (88 pp)

VOLUME IV (1973)

01-037	W. A. Cornelius, Political Learning Among the Migrant Poor: Impact of Residential Context (88 pp)	
01-038	J. W. White, Political Implications of Cityward Migration: Japan as An Exploratory Test Case (64 pp)	
01-039	R. B. Stauffer, Nation-Building in a Global Economy: the Role of the Multinational Corporation (48 pp)	
01-040	A. Martin, The Politics of Economic Policy in the United States: A Tentative View from a Comparative Perspective (64 pp)	
01-041	M. B. Welfling, Political Institutionalization: Comparative Analysis of African Party Systems (72pp)	$
01-042	B. Ames, Rhetoric and Reality in a Militarized Regime: Brazil Since 1964 (56pp)	$
01-043	E. C. Browne, Coalition Theories (96pp)	$
01-044	M. Barrera, Information and Ideology: A Study of Arturo Frondizi (52pp)	$
01-045	Murphy et al, Public Evaluations of Constitutional Courts (64pp)	$
01-046	R. A. Lane, Political Man: Toward a Conceptual Base (72 pp)	$
01-047	W. R. Thompson, The Grievances of Military Coup-Makers (76 pp)	$
01-048	P. Fagen, Chilean Universities: Problems of Autonomy and Dependence (52 pp)	$

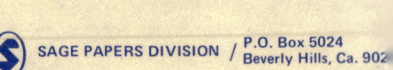

SAGE PAPERS DIVISION / P.O. Box 5024
Beverly Hills, Ca. 902

PROFESSIONAL PAPER **SUBSCRIPTION** INFORMATION APPEARS ELSEWHERE ON THIS CAR

PIC 374/2

Sage Research Papers in the Social Sciences

The *Sage Research Papers in the Social Sciences* series makes available from one source an outstanding collection of original papers in a variety of subfields—selected by several different sponsoring organizations or institutions. The sponsor and series' editors for these papers are listed below. In 1974 approximately eight additional, distinguished institutions will serve as sponsors for further subseries.

Ordering Information

As Separates: Papers may be purchased separately. Depending on length, they are priced at $2.50 or $3.00 each. Orders totaling less than $10.00 must be accompanied by payment.

On Subscription: Subscriptions will be accepted for Volumes 1 and 2, 1973-1974, comprising 40 papers. The subscription price is $80.00, compared with a single-copy price of at least $100.00.

*STUDIES IN COMPARATIVE MODERNIZATION SERIES
  Sponsored by the Harry S Truman Institute, The Hebrew University of Jerusalem
  Series Editors: S. N. Eisenstadt and D. Weintraub

+COMPARATIVE LEGISLATIVE STUDIES SERIES
  Sponsored by the Consortium for Comparative Legislative Research (Duke University, The University of Hawaii, The University of Iowa, and State University of New York at Albany)
  Series Editor: Malcolm E. Jewell

VOLUME I (1973)

90-001	*D. Weintraub, Development and Modernization in the Philippines (32pp)	$2.50
90-002	+A. Kornberg et al, Legislatures and Societal Change: The Case of Canada (64pp)	$2.50
90-003	*S. N. Eisenstadt, Traditional Patrimonialism and Modern Neopatrimonialism (96pp)	$3.00
90-004	+J. E. Hakes, Weak Parliaments and Military Coups in Africa (40pp)	$2.50
90-005	*R. Kahane, The Problem of Political Legitimacy in an Antagonistic Society: The Indonesian Case (52pp)	$2.50
90-006	+J. G. Grumm, A Paradigm for the Comparative Analysis of Legislative Systems (84pp)	$3.00
90-007	+S. W. Hughes and K. J. Mijeski, Legislative-Executive Policy-Making (60pp)	$3.00
90-008	*B. Kimmerling and M. Lissak, Inner-Dualism: An Outcome of the Center-Periphery Relationship During Modernization Processes in Uganda (44pp)	$2.50

VOLUME II (1974)

90-009	*Y. Levy, Malaysia and Ceylon: A Study of Two Developing Centres	$2.50
90-010	+N. Meller, Institutional Adaptability: Legislative Reference in Japan and the United States	$3.00

Thirty additional titles to be announced

 SAGE PAPERS DIVISION / P.O. Box 5024, Beverly Hills, Ca. 90210

SAGE PROFESSIONAL PAPERS
■■■ GENERAL INFORMATION FOR ALL SERIES ■■■

These series are designed with both research and classroom usage in mind; papers are available either on subscription (assuring quick receipt of timely work in the field—as well as savings of up to 50% over single copy prices) or as single titles for personal or classroom use (priced at $2.00 to $3.00 each, depending on length). Papers range in length from 32 to 96 pages; articles are published which are too long for normal journal publication, yet too short to become books.

Frequency: twelve papers per year in each series, published in groups of four throughout the year.

Paper Edition, Unbound – Subscription Rates (for each series)

	one year	two year	three year
Institutional	$21.00	$41.00	$60.00
Individual	$12.00	$23.00	$33.00

Subscription discounts to professionals and students are granted ONLY on orders paid by personal check or money order. Wherever possible, payment should accompany orders, since service will not begin until payment has been received.

Outside the U.S. and Canada, add $1.00 per year to above rates.

ask your librarian to order today!

Bound Library Edition Available in three clothbound parts (each containing four papers) per year (in each series).

Subscription Price $30 per year (i.e., $10 per bound part) for each series.

Regular Price $37.50 per annual volume (i.e., $12.50 per bound part)—if bound parts are ordered separately, or after publication.

Outside the U.S. and Canada, add $3.00 per volume (or $1.00 per part) to the above rates.

What is a SAGE PROFESSIONAL PAPER?

According to CHOICE (a magazine of the American Library Association) — when reviewing our series of professional papers in comparative politics — it's a "most valuable, inexpensive... outlet for research products" which provides "specialists with high quality monographs too narrow and short to appear as full-length books and rather too long to be published in academic journals... An extremely useful library acquisition."

ASK YOUR LIBRARIAN TO ORDER ALL THESE IMPORTANT SERIES TODAY !!!

SAGE PROFESSIONAL PAPERS IN
Administrative and Policy Studies

Editor: H. George Frederickson, *Indiana University*

Includes both theoretical and empirical works in business and public administration—as well as the other social science disciplines—as they bear on policy-making and policy implementation. In addition, research and theory on the internal behavior of complex organizations will be regularly published.

VOLUME I

03-001	E. Ostrom, et al., Community Organization and the Provision of Police Services (96 pp)	$3.00
03-002	R. S. Ahlbrandt, Jr., Municipal Fire Protection Services: Comparison of Alternative Organizational Forms (72 pp)	$2.70
03-003	D. O. Porter, et al., The Politics of Budgeting Federal Aid: Resource Mobilization by Local School Districts (96 pp)	$3.00
03-004	J. P. Viteritti, Police, Politics, and Pluralism in New York City: A Comparative Case Study (72 pp)	$2.70
03-005	R. L. Schott, Professionals in Public Service: The Characteristics and Education of Engineer Federal Executives (64pp)	$2.50
03-006	C. Argyris, On Organizations of the Future (56pp)	$2.40
03-007	O. White, Jr., Psychic Energy and Organizational Change (48pp)	$2.25
03-008	D. C. Perry et al, Politics at the Street Level (40pp)	$2.10
03-009	H. Margolis, Technical Advice on Policy Issues (64pp)	$2.40
03-010	M. Holden, Jr., The Politics of Poor Relief (48pp)	$2.10
03-011	S. Nagel, Minimizing Costs and Maximizing Benefits in Providing Legal Services to the Poor (56pp)	$2.25
03-012	Y. H. Cho and H. G. Frederickson, Determinants of Public Policy in the American States (64pp)	$2.40

Forthcoming...

VOLUME II (1974)

03-013	C. Altenstetter, Health Policy Making and Administration in West Germany and the U.S.	$3.00*
03-014	L. J. Lundquist, Environmental Policies in Canada, Sweden, and the U.S.	$2.50*
03-015	G. D. Garson, On Democratic Administration and Socialist Self-Management: A Comparative Survey Emphasizing the Yugoslav Experience	$2.50*
03-016	W. B. Eimicke, Public Administration in a Democratic Context: Theory and Practice	$3.00*
03-017	R. Robarts, French Development Assistance	$3.00*
03-018	H. V. Savitch and M. W. Adler, Decentralization at the Grassroots	$2.50*

*denotes tentative prices

SAGE PROFESSIONAL PAPERS IN
American Politics

Editor: Randall B. Ripley, *Ohio State University*

A new and flexible outlet for high quality social science stud[ies in] any aspect of American politics. Papers will focus on empiri[cal] research, methodological questions, or theoretical concerns [on] such varied topics as public policy, political parties, public o[pin]ion, political socialization, legislative or judicial behavior, th[e] legal process, urban, state and federal politics.

VOLUME I (1973)

04-001	S. S. Nagel, Comparing Elected and Appointed Judicial Systems (48 pp)	
04-002	J. Dennis, Political Socialization Research: A Bibliography (56 pp)	
04-003	H. B. Asher, Freshman Representatives and the Learning of Voting Cues (64 pp)	
04-004	J. Fishel, Representation and Responsiveness in Congress: The "Class of Eighty-Nine," 1965-1970 (72 pp)	
04-005	R. Abrams, Some Conceptual Problems of Voting Theory (52pp)	
04-006	R. Ripley et al, Structure, Environment and Policy Actions (60pp)	
04-007	P. Burgess and R. Conway, Public Goods and Voluntary Associations: A Multi-State Investigation of Collective Action in Labor Union Locals (56pp)	
04-008	P. Hill, A Theory of Political Coalitions in Simple and Policy-Making Situations (64pp)	
04-009	H. Asher and D. Van Meter, Determinants of Public Welfare Policies (64pp)	
04-010	E. C. Ladd, Jr., and C. Hadley, Political Parties and Political Issues: Patterns in Differentiation Since the New Deal (88pp)	
04-011	C. A. Broh, Toward a Theory of Issue Voting (36pp)	
04-012	T. Ball, Civil Disobedience and Civil Deviance (56pp)	

VOLUME II (1974)

04-013	T. H. Roback, Recruitment and Incentive Patterns Among Grassroots Republican Officials	
04-014	P. L. Beardsley et al, Measuring Public Opinion on Priorities	

*denotes tentative p[rices]

PROFESSIONAL PAPER SUBSCRIPTION INFORMATION APPEARS ELSEWHERE ON THIS CAR[D]

MAIL TO
SAGE Publications / P.O. Box 5024 / Beverly Hills, Calif. 90210
orders from the U.K., Europe, the Middle East and Africa
should be sent to 44 Hatton Garden, London EC1N 8ER

PIC 374/6